Henry Stanley Newman

Banani

the transition from slavery to freedom in Zanzibar and Pemba

Henry Stanley Newman

Banani
the transition from slavery to freedom in Zanzibar and Pemba

ISBN/EAN: 9783744741279

Printed in Europe, USA, Canada, Australia, Japan

Cover: Foto ©ninafisch / pixelio.de

More available books at **www.hansebooks.com**

BANANI:

The Transition from Slavery to Freedom in Zanzibar and Pemba.

BY

HENRY STANLEY NEWMAN,

Editor of "The Friend,"
Author of "Palestine Lessons," "Christian Solidarity," etc.

London:
HEADLEY BROTHERS, 14, BISHOPSGATE STREET WITHOUT, E.C.
Leominster:
THE ORPHANS' PRINTING PRESS, BROAD STREET.

LEOMINSTER:
THE ORPHANS' PRINTING PRESS,
BROAD STREET.

INTRODUCTORY.

I GLADLY express my gratitude to the author for having interested himself, and the public through the medium of this book, in matters pertaining to the population in the island of Pemba.

The blot that has attached to our nation so long in maintaining the recognition of slavery on the island of Pemba, and throughout the Zanzibar Protectorate, is now being obliterated. The evils due to the system cannot at once be removed. It is to be done by work such as that alluded to in this book, which will, I trust, do much to assist the authorities in solving their difficulties, and gradually raising the moral tone of the negro population and of their masters, who have been degraded by association with slavery.

JOSEPH A. PEASE.

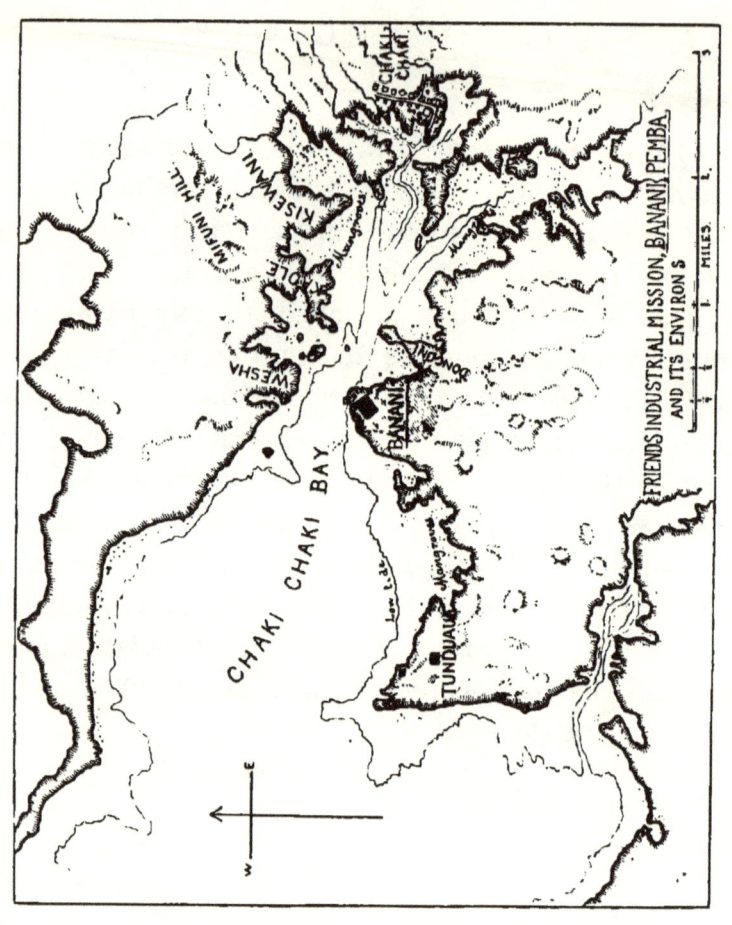

PREFACE.

The eyes of the civilised world turn to Africa with ever-increasing interest. It was my privilege in the spring of 1897 to accompany Theodore Burtt to East Africa, Zanzibar, and Pemba, and to gain some little insight into the actual working of slavery on the eve of the important juncture of the abolition of the legal status in those islands.

We received unfailing courtesy from the officials of the Government, and our thanks are due to General Sir Lloyd William Mathews, to Consul-General Sir Arthur Hardinge, to Vice-Consul D. R. O'Sullivan, to Mr. Herbert Lister, and others, both in Mombasa, Zanzibar, and Pemba, who furthered our inquiries, and gave us every assistance in their power. With introductions from the authorities in Zanzibar, we made the acquaintance of leading Arab sheikhs on the island of Pemba, and visited a number of shambas and plantations on both islands.

The discussion of the intricate problem of emancipation may prove the means of a clearer understanding in England of the issues involved. One of the services of history is to enable men to realise how many social victories have already been won. The extinction of slave-raiding and of slave caravans in the East Africa Protectorate is a great achievement. It was in 1873 that Bishop Steere wrote home exultingly: "The last open slave market in the world has just been closed." The annihilation of the slave trade in Zanzibar, except possibly an occasional instance of smuggling, is another advance. Cruelty cannot exult with open face, as of yore. The condition of the slaves is better. Thus history kindles hope, and hope inspires further effort. But so long as slavery exists, prosperity is exiled. Justice demands that every man, woman, and child, not convicted of crime, shall be free. Justice delayed is injustice.

The despatch of Lord Salisbury last February, initiating the abolition of the legal status of slavery, marks an important epoch in the forward movement. At first it seemed that month by month slaves were being liberated; more recently we heard of slaves being sent back to their masters, and a steady backwater of moral inertia seemed to have set in. Now, through the renewed activity of the English officials, the tide of deliverance is, we trust, rising again; but it is evident that much more definite work remains to be done.

The current of thought in the following pages is toward further work and fuller emancipation. The spirit of Christianity leavening social life can alone really emancipate Africa. Africa is for the Africans, but we firmly believe that Africa needs Europe to succour and direct her. It is not the interest of the negroes or of the Arabs exclusively that has to be consulted. No fairer spots on earth are found than the coral islands of Zanzibar and Pemba, their hills clothed with fronded palms and spicy groves. Pemba is called by the Arabs Jazirat-el-Khazra, the Emerald Isle. Although morally so dark, it is the pearl of the Indian Ocean.

The aim of the Friends' Industrial Mission at Banani, on Pemba, is in every way in its power to uphold and assist the Government in carrying out in its integrity the decree for the abolition of the legal status of slavery, and to loyally second its efforts in that direction. It is useless to cover up or ignore the very serious difficulties that surround abolition in the character of the peoples affected by the change. We have confidence in the English officials who have charge of the subject. But it is a work that must take time for readjustment. The ultimate result can only be the full emancipation of the negro race within the whole of our Protectorates.

HENRY STANLEY NEWMAN.

Leominster,
    January, 1898.

OLD SUGAR FACTORY, BANANI.

H. Armitage, Photo.

CONTENTS.

CHAPTER	PAGE
I. THE TRANSITION	1
II. NATURAL RESOURCES	13
III. SLAVERY AS IT WAS	29
IV. THE AFRICAN AS A SOCIAL FACTOR	40
V. THE ARAB AS A SOCIAL FACTOR	50
VI. THE HINDU AS A SOCIAL FACTOR	67
VII. THE ENGLISH AS A SOCIAL FACTOR	75
VIII. GOVERNMENT BY PROTECTORATE	87
IX. THE WIDER OUTLOOK	101
X. THE ABOLITION OF THE LEGAL STATUS OF SLAVERY	111
XI. EAST AFRICA PROTECTORATE	125
XII. EXISTING MISSIONARY WORK	143
XIII. FRIENDS' INDUSTRIAL MISSION, BANANI	159
XIV. THE WORKING OF THE DECREE	177

APPENDIX :—

Instructions to Mr. Hardinge respecting the Abolition of the Legal Status of Slavery in the Islands of Zanzibar and Pemba .   199

Mr. Hardinge's Reply 210

The Sultan's Decree Abolishing the Legal Status of Slavery in Zanzibar and Pemba .   210

INDEX .   213

ILLUSTRATIONS.

	PAGE
MAP OF THE EAST AFRICA PROTECTORATE AND UGANDA	*Frontispiece*
MAP OF FRIENDS' INDUSTRIAL MISSION, BANANI, AND ITS ENVIRONS	iv.
OLD SUGAR FACTORY, BANANI	viii.
THE SULTAN'S PALACE, ZANZIBAR	3
GENERAL SIR L. W. MATHEWS	9
TROPICAL VEGETATION	15
ROCK PINNACLES, ZANZIBAR	19
GATHERING CLOVES, ZANZIBAR	24
LIFE ON THE SHAMBA	28
SLAVE GIRLS, WATER-CARRIERS OF ZANZIBAR	35
NATIVE BOYS AND GIRLS AND HUTS, ZANZIBAR	41
CUSTOM-HOUSE, CHAKI-CHAKI, PEMBA	46
MARKET-PLACE, CHAKI-CHAKI, PEMBA	53
ZANZIBAR ARABS	58
THE CASTLE, CHAKI-CHAKI, PEMBA	64
THE PARSI CLUB, ZANZIBAR	69
A STREET SCENE IN CHAKI-CHAKI, PEMBA	73
ZANZIBAR	78
STREET SCENE, ZANZIBAR	83
SLAVE GIRL BUYING FRUIT FROM HINDU TRADESMAN	88
ON THE SHAMBA	92
SCENE ON PLANTATION	96
DRYING CLOVES AT BANANI	100
CHAKI-CHAKI, PEMBA	106
BANANI ESTATE, LOOKING ACROSS BAY	110
MAKUTI HUTS ON FRIENDS' ESTATE, BANANI	116
OUR RESIDENCE IN CHAKI-CHAKI	122
MOMBASA HARBOUR	128
UGANDA RAILWAY, KILINDINI, MOMBASA	135
CHURCH MISSIONARY HOUSE, FRERETOWN	142
CITY OF ZANZIBAR, FROM THE SHAMBA	148
CATHEDRAL OF UNIVERSITIES' MISSION, ZANZIBAR	155
DIGGING FOUNDATIONS OF MISSION HOUSE AT BANANI	160
BANANI	165
THE PATH UP FROM THE SHORE, BANANI	171
"THE FRIEND OF PEMBA" MISSION BOAT	175
MOMBASA HARBOUR, FROM MISSION HOUSE, FRERETOWN	179
MISSION WORK, FRERETOWN	183
MARKET, CHRISTIAN VILLAGE, FRERETOWN	187
THE MOMBASA-UGANDA RAILWAY	191
GROUP OF NATIVES, BANANI	194
RUIN ON THE SHORE, BANANI	198

CHAPTER I.

THE TRANSITION.

"Kulla mlango na ufunguo wakwe" ("Every door has its key").—
Swahili Proverb.

THE transition through which the islands of Zanzibar and Pemba are passing is conspicuous in the city of Zanzibar itself and in its harbour. No one can thoughtfully take a bird's-eye view of the scene presented from any prominent position without seeing around him signs of change and of progress. Through the kind hospitality of Captain Agnew, I lodged in the highest room in Zanzibar, christened by our generous friend, General Sir W. L. Mathews, as "*Mnara-ne*" (Swahili for "in the Tower"). From this vantage ground, at the top of several flights of stairs, with eight windows, looking north, south, east, and west, and the sea spread out before me on three sides, I had plenty to remind me of the transformation that is coming over East Africa. The high hills of the German Protectorate on the mainland skirted the horizon in a long line to the westward, beyond the little green islands that studded the sea like emeralds. Arab dhows, mail steamers, and men-of-war lay anchored in the bays immediately in front, the dhows carrying the flags of various nations—Persian, German, French, English, as well as the crimson flag of the Sultan, each dhow "protected" by the Power whose flag its owner elected to sail under. In the midst of these representatives of various nationalities, the three masts of the Sultan's steamer, the *Glasgow*, that was sunk during the bombardment in 1896, stood up out of the water. Those three masts were a weird reminder of the great change that had taken place in the last few months. The bombardment only continued forty minutes; but as the eye ran along the shore-line to the north of the English Consulate, its effects were seen in the dilapidated Palace. For some months the local authorities had been carting away the ruins, and the unsightly wreck of the neighbouring houses took long to remove. The Palace was looted, but is being rebuilt, the old buildings along the sea-front are being cleared away, and the stone-work is being used to fill up an ugly salt-water lagoon that must long have been a hot-bed of malaria in the native quarter. The city of Zanzibar itself is full of interest. It is undoubtedly the metropolis of East Africa. No town or city from Natal to Aden can dispute its pre-eminence. To the Germans it is an important commercial centre, and there is a large German Club, as well as the German Consulate. One of the conspicuous buildings in the city is the cathedral of the Universities' Mission, erected on the site of the old slave market, which was closed in 1873. Near the cathedral cluster a number of mission buildings that are a hive of industry, philanthropy, and light. In the centre of the city the French Catholics are erecting a large cathedral of their own.

From our outlook in the *Mnara-ne* we see the little narrow alleys that do duty for streets in Zanzibar, and there lie below us acres of flat roofs, with small wooden look-outs and shelters erected on them. The palm trees, with here and there a mango or orange tree, oleanders, and groups of bananas, add picturesqueness to the scene; while immediately below us, from the tall warehouses, may be seen a

THE SULTAN'S PALACE, ZANZIBAR, 1896.

group of slave-porters with burdens on their heads, marching in single file, singing some native Swahili chorus as they toil. The air is very clear; there is not the smoky atmosphere that disfigures English cities, but it is a dreamy, tropical landscape in the hot glare of the sun, so that the eye turns willingly to the pleasant green clove plantations inland, or the bright blue waters along the shore. Remarkable freaks of nature are to be seen here and there. Hidden away to the south is a gorge hollowed out by the monsoons, with pillars of rock left standing like statues. The pinnacles are composed of sandstone, but have the appearance of drapery hanging in long flowing robes of grey cloth, and present a strange spectacle. Everything around us is in transition, and of all the elements which greet us among a people religiously opposed to change, there is no greater or more far-reaching change than the emancipation of the negro from the bondage of centuries. The Government has, with a variety of limitations and cautionary provisions, abolished the legal status of slavery. It is therefore desirable that we should comprehend the circumstances—natural, social, and historical—that must to a large extent mould the future.

On our arrival in Zanzibar in January, 1897, we found a remarkable consensus of opinion existing among thoughtful people that emancipation lay straight before them as the programme of the future, the only questions being as to *how* and *when* it should be accomplished. In every movement there are advocates for sudden and definite changes, while others prefer gradual evolution. But it is never right to abandon evil by degrees. The sooner a wrong is righted the better. Thoughtful people know well that much preparation precedes the crisis, that no one day or hour merits all the honour of a great step forward, that there is much that has to take place (and probably takes place slowly) both before and after the Rubicon is crossed.

One line of thought in this connection impresses observers with regard to slavery in these islands, and that is a fact that lies on the surface, yet has been far too much ignored in England—that *a great deal had already been accomplished* in these islands in the direction of emancipation before any edict of emancipation found utterance. It is probably so in every social or political reform; yet in the heat of debate, the years of quiet, onward preparation are too often ignored. Thus we might mark dates in our own visit, and say that on the 20th January we landed in Zanzibar; on the 24th January we reached Tunduaua, on the island of Pemba; that on the 27th January we entered the house which the Zanzibar Government had generously provided and furnished for us at Chaki-Chaki. But such a calendar conveys little to the reader of months of quiet thought and growing conviction, or the chain of kind providences that attended our journeyings; and how little such dates convey of the merest beginnings of movements that we hope in after years may be fruitful in good results! Let it then be fairly recognised that many steps had already been taken by our English Government and by the responsible officials in Zanzibar, that materially ameliorated the actual condition of the slaves, affecting the whole area of slavery, and preparing the way for complete emancipation.

Slavery is an ugly thing at best. It is bad in itself, and must vanish before Christianity. But the presence of wise and watchful officials is helpful in restraining the iniquities that attach to an institution that has long been condemned as intolerable by enlightened nations. Such ameliorating influences by no means cover all the good already done in Zanzibar. The suppression of the slave trade between the mainland and Zanzibar had been aimed at, and to a considerable extent achieved. Cases of the smuggling of slaves still occasionally occurred, but undoubtedly the wholesale import of slaves formerly carried on had ceased. The hemming in of slavery by laws with regard to slaves being inherited resulted in not a few obtaining their freedom. The fact that children seven years of age were free prevented the legal accession to slavery by the natural law of increase, although the Agreement was often practically ignored. The vigilance of Government officials in dealing with cases of cruelty, where proved, acted most usefully as a deterrent to hard-hearted Arabs.

The extinction of slavery is a work of time and plodding effort; the whole system of slavery is too deeply ingrained in the social inner life of Africa to be quickly eradicated. England and English officials hate any appearance of a mere paper reform. What our Government announces it endeavours to carry out. The good we would accomplish may fall short of our ideal, but our aim is, not to announce an ideal without an honest struggle to make it a realisation. We believe there had been an honest effort to make previous edicts effectual in Zanzibar; but the duplicate form of government, nominally by a Sultan, actually by British officials, did not make it easy to give effect to edicts which might be edicts of a Sultan, or stipulations between our Government and the Sultan, and were much more easily inscribed and sealed on parchment than made practically effectual among the people.

God has many ways of working. He is not narrowed or limited to proclamations, edicts, or decrees. Many influences in active operation in society and in commercial relationships are more potent than edicts. Injustice is a boomerang which returns home on the unjust. Academic debates have taken place as to whether slavery is good or ill for certain races and low conditions of men. But far above the small talk of such debates is the hand of God in history. The challenge comes from on high, to dynasties and nations, "Let my people go." The night on which Israel crossed the Red Sea was a night to be much remembered, but it was a night preceded by terrible plagues. America was plagued with a fearful civil war before the nation, religiously professing liberty, set free five million slaves. The plague was great, but after the sacrifice of the lives of hundreds of thousands of American citizens in a fratricidal civil war deliverance came, and was wafted from the cotton mills of Massachusetts to the pine forests of Alabama.

We find a similar nemesis working to-day in Zanzibar and Pemba. The power of the Arab is paralysed by debt. The Hindu mortgage-monger has his hard knuckle on the throat of the slave-holder. The trade in cloves, that a few years ago was a source of rapid wealth, has a plague upon it. The commercial crisis is so great, that while Government receives nearly two-thirds of its revenue from the intensely fertile island of Pemba, it knows that, unless some great change takes place, the trade of the island that has laid the golden eggs is *in extremis*. The plague that precedes emancipation in a form adapted to circumstances was resting on Pemba. Though there was in the Divine hand a rod, it was the rod of deliverance. The *only* pathway open was emancipation.

It is delusive to search for precedents of the position of things here. God is far too rich in resourcefulness. History is too full of fresh inspiration to exactly duplicate itself. There are parallelisms in human affairs that are of value, that mark the workings of one Mind, but there is an infinite variety in the many fulfilments of one Law. The history of emancipation in the West Indies is instructive respecting our present problem in Zanzibar and Pemba, but the two cases are singularly different. There we had for generations the influences of Christian missionaries and of some form of Christian government. Here we are dealing with an institution that, whatever the Koran or Islam authorities may lay down, is unfortunately generally linked with Mohammedan sway. Certainly their code of morality is not ours. Power is not given to us in order that we may enable them to continue their iniquities. The Arabs are not likely again lightly to challenge the decision of England. Our rule in these islands is much more pronounced than ever before.

While, however, Zanzibar and the West Indies are essentially different, one illustration, that of Antigua, may inspire courage in the hearts of any who fear the results of emancipation in Zanzibar. The following facts are marked in the history of Antigua, and are confirmed by a variety of evidence from the commercial men of the island. The transition from slavery to freedom effected a great change for the better in the condition of the negroes. Emancipation was the result of political and pecuniary considerations, rather than of religious principle. The event took place peaceably on one day (the 1st August, 1834). After emancipation there was no rebellion. Emancipation was regarded by all classes as a blessing. Free labour was found to be less wasteful than slave labour. The negroes did their work more cheerfully and

Gomez, Photo.

GENERAL SIR W. L. MATHEWS.

better, and were more easily managed as free men. They became more trustworthy, taking a deeper interest in the affairs of their employers. Antigua proves that emancipated slaves appreciate law. They have shown no disposition to roam from place to place. Freedom suddenly bestowed did not make the negroes more insolent. The freed negroes proved that they were able to take care of themselves. Emancipation tended to elevate the men, and effected a vast improvement in the condition of the women. Real estate rose in value.*

Such thoughts bring us to the practical outcome of the present movement. Sir Arthur Hardinge has, in his despatches, repeatedly referred to the trend of events as a "transition." Transition not only includes much that goes before and prepares the way, but it includes *much that must follow after*. We rejoice in the careful thought the home Government, as well as the officials in Zanzibar, have given to future needs. With the best intentions, the supreme inertia and the adherence to custom animating Oriental peoples make advancement *slow*. The emancipation of a composite community from the customs of their forefathers is not to be suddenly effected by an edict of the Sultan, or by a message from Downing Street. A decree changes the legal status of the slave, but no decree can suddenly transform his character. Mr. Burt, of the Church Missionary Society, as he took us through the streets of Mombasa on our way to Zanzibar, said the great philosophy of life in Africa might be embodied in one word, "*pola, pola!*" ("slowly, slowly"). Dr. Edwards added: "Yes, you may take that as the key to maintaining your health; but

* See Thorne and Kimball's "Report of Emancipation in the West Indies."

you may take it also as the key to your missionary success. Take things quietly; you must in Africa be willing to make progress slowly." If we truly recognise the progress that had previously been made, we shall be the better prepared to look hopefully on much that remains to be done.

We have to consider how to help the negro to make the right use of emancipation, how to enable him to rise to the emergency of "independence." He is very low down and degraded at present. But the progress he has made in the United States in intelligence, in educational acquisition, in religious faith, and in administrative power, shows the immense capacity in negro races to rise. That he has risen in contact with the white man in America is an argument that he can rise in the social scale in the tropics. The tropical climate, that steals the energy from the European, has not an equal effect upon the African. He is in his natural habitat. Here he can physically thrive. The deterioration that has marked both the Arab and the negro under slavery need not be permanent under emancipation. But if there is one thing more than another which the negro at present lacks, it is the capacity to be independent. He needs some superior race alongside him to enable him to rise. Under slavery the Arab taught the negro to sink his manliness, and the negro woman to prostitute her home life. But as the purer influences of English life appear upon the scene, the negro will rise in the presence of the higher aims of Christian civilization. Missionaries are a great help in this direction; but true missionary work among the negro races must not be one-sided. The cultivation and the concurrent development of the *hand*, the *head*, and the *heart*, are essential.

The present degradation is so great, that the elevation of the race must be accompanied with great patience. The husbandman that labours to make the barren ground fruitful, by tillage and by seed-sowing, works by faith, expecting the harvest hereafter. So let us work expectantly and patiently.

It was at sunrise on a lovely Sabbath morning that the *Barawa* cast anchor in Chaki-Chaki Bay, off Pemba. The sails had been set to the breeze that wafted us along, and the same breeze was swaying the fronds of the tall cocoanut palms that guarded the shore at Tunduaua as the black boys rowed us to the beach. The natives, with true appreciation, have named the spot Tunduaua, "the beautiful place like a flower," with its thousand acres of mangoes, cloves, and palms. A sheltering cloud, protecting from the heat of the sun, has been kindly granted to Pemba, and this cloud morning by morning rests over the island. But from under the cloud, and behind the long line of tropical verdure that fringed the coast, the sun shone out upon us, like a forecast of the brighter day about to break upon the swarthy cultivators among these luxuriant plantations. Instead of the cloud of slavery, with all its depressing influences, there has risen upon these people the morning star of freedom. As we enter upon the consideration of the various forces that go to mould the future of East Africa, we must remember that it is the *formation of character* that can alone secure permanent success, and that can alone gild the horizon with hope.

CHAPTER II.

NATURAL RESOURCES.

"Fishing in deep water requires skilled workmen."—*Swahili Proverb*.

ISLANDS have played a remarkable part in the destiny of nations. The British Isles have dominated the world, peopling new empires and colonies in the West, controlling the future of the East in India, establishing vast protectorates in Africa. The island city of Venice dominated Italy; and the astute Arabs founded their power in East Africa by making the islands, and especially the island of Zanzibar, their base of operations.

In considering the natural resources of Zanzibar and Pemba, we must bear in mind that both are formed from end to end of coral. Other formations crop up here and there. The east coast is swept by periodical ocean storms, and the coral rag in many cases is scoured of such soil as might otherwise accumulate. A dense low scrub covers much of these eastern tracts of country.

Zanzibar is fifty-five miles long, twenty miles across in its widest part, and about eighteen miles from the mainland. The island of Pemba is thirty miles to the north of the island of Zanzibar, and is some forty miles long, and eight to twelve miles in width. The areas of greatest fertility are the slopes which lie to the west of the long ranges of hills running down the centre of the islands. Here mile after mile of clove trees and of cocoanut palms crowd the landscape. The country is beautifully undulating, and though the hills are not more than from 100ft. to 200ft. high, the contour of the whole is one unbroken succession of hills and valleys, clothed with tropical verdure from summit to base. On Zanzibar an excellent Government road runs across the island; but on Pemba there are no roads except rough foot-tracks throughout the island. The only exception is a road recently made by the Government from the shore, of less than a mile, to the estate it has acquired. With the exception of a few donkeys used for transport purposes, everything on Pemba in the way of produce is carried on the heads of the negroes.

On the plantations of these islands there are not only tens of thousands of clove trees and cocoanut palms, but betel-nut palms, oil palms, date palms, silk cotton trees 60ft. to 80ft. high, oranges and citrons, pomegranates, mangoes, custard apples, papaw, pomelo, jack-fruit, guava, banana, cassava, and sugar-cane. Chillies, pepper, annatto, and pine-apples grow abundantly, and appear to be indigenous; while in cultivation there are cinnamon, coffee, nutmegs, and vanilla. The Zanzibar Government has established three experimental farms as nursery grounds for new products. Two of these are on the island of Zanzibar, namely, Dunga, under the care of Mr. Lyne, the Director of Agriculture; and Chwaka, under the care of Mr. J. T. Last, R.G.S. The plantation on the island of Pemba is Tunduaua, the residence of Mr. Farler and Mr. Herbert Lister.

Through the kindness of Dr. A. H. Spurrier, formerly editor of the *Zanzibar Gazette*, I visited the aboriginal fortress and palace of Dunga. The new road is a great credit to the Sultanate, and opens up a very valuable tract of country. Houses are springing up along the route, and there are evidences of an increase of prosperity and of traffic.

TROPICAL VEGETATION.

We rested half-way at a lovely bungalow by the river side, round which were flourishing the most brilliantly coloured crotons. The children were bathing among the tall reeds in the river, while the purple water-lilies half concealed the fish that sheltered under the flat leaves. Round the bungalow were growing choice vines and fairy-like creepers, whose gorgeous blossoms hung with delicious negligence in the sunshine, their stamens drooping from them like jewelled earrings. At this half-way village a long bridge takes us across the largest river on the island. A rice swamp runs along the river valley. Across this we struck eastward for seven miles, up and down hill, through clove plantations and across waste commons spangled with flowers. Dunga originally belonged to the Sultan of the Wahadimu people. It stands on a very fertile plateau above the surrounding valleys that run longitudinally north and south. It is called a palace or fortress, and was held for generations by the aborigines, who appear never to have been conquered by the Arabs. The wall that surrounded the palace yard as a defence is still in several places standing, and encloses not only the courtyard but large gardens. The mortar with which the walls were constructed is very hard, and I was informed that the native Sultan who erected the walls had ordered a number of his slaves to be killed in order that their blood might be mixed with the mortar to make it cohere more firmly. Such is the cruel disregard of human life begotten of the great scourge of Africa! The house is to some extent modernised and rebuilt, but has a handsome old central staircase of Oriental construction, and many of the apartments are protected with strong masonry; some of which are said to be haunted. There are very fine views from the spacious flat roof. But the whole bears the appearance of a large old farmhouse rather than of a palace, and the exterior is very plain. Within the courtyard grows the remarkable durian tree, whose fruit has a most disagreeable odour. A large nutmeg tree stands close by, on which the nutmegs are hanging. In the gardens are rows of the ornamental betel-nut palm, large quantities of vanilla vines, and hundreds of young indiarubber plants which have been recently planted.

At Tunduaua oranges and limes grow freely in the enclosure immediately in front of the verandah, and were in blossom and in fruit when we landed. Coffee and vanilla flourish. From the verandah, which is raised two or three feet from the ground, we look out through the tall palms on to the blue ocean. The house contains three central apartments for Europeans, with side rooms for servants, the house standing like a square salt-box, with no glass in the windows, but iron bars to prevent ingress. High above the house rises the great overhanging roof, with abundance of open space for fresh air between the roof and the ceilings. The rafters for the roof are made of long bamboo poles, which grow abundantly on the islands. These are covered with shrewdly plaited palm leaves, which are compacted together and stretch over the verandahs, forming the universal *makuti* roof of plantation life. A tarriance in such surroundings convinces a visitor of the magnificent natural resources of the islands, in the abundant harvest which is month after month being gathered from the exuberant vegetation. Every little hilltop abounds with the fronded palms or the green bushy mangoes, the slopes being clothed with the shining clove trees; while the fertile valleys lend themselves to the easy cultivation of the little hoes of the coloured men and women, resulting in luxuriant crops of sugar-cane, m'hogo, rice, maize, and pulse. Nature is very lavish in the tropics in satisfying the needs of man, while the climate induces *ennui* and exhaustion, and an incapacity to accomplish the energetic work of northern latitudes. There are, however, abundant compensations in the bountiful prodigality of the spices and the fruit which the tall trees that fan the languid air are laying at our feet.

We visited the east coast of Pemba in company with Consul O'Sullivan and an experienced Arab, but had to leave our donkeys behind us long before we could reach the shore, and performed the remainder of the journey on foot along a very narrow track shaded with tall dense bushes, in which were beautiful tropical butterflies and insects; but there seemed nothing but the rough ragged coral under our feet, harder than any ordinary rock, and presenting a sharp, jagged surface. Passing along this fisherman's track, we reached the shore, where the rock overhanging the beach was worn away by the waves into caves and hollows. Crested breakers were tossing over the long reef out to sea.

The west coast is very different. It is indented with a multitude of creeks and bays, protected from the sea by a necklace of coral reefs and isles that form a natural breakwater. No coast in the world seemed naturally more adapted than Pemba for running in slaves from the mainland. Up the long creeks, fringed with mangroves, the Arab traders could run their dhows at high tide. The trees grow in the quiet salt water, covered above the tide-line with foliage, and the entrances to these creeks are often so entangled with shoals and with vegetation that no stranger can safely approach. When English vessels appeared, and the process of pre-

PILLARS OF ROCK, ZANZIBAR. (SEE PAGE 4.)

venting the slave trade was undertaken by European philanthropy, only a very small proportion of the slaves could be intercepted in transit. More efficacious remedies for the slave trade have now been devised, and the long reaches of smooth water within the shelter of the coral reefs are destined by a kindly providence to higher and happier service.

The harvest of the sea in these shallow lagoons is the delight of the negro population. On our voyage to Weti we passed scores of people standing in the most grotesque attitudes in the water, gathering shell-fish. The low reaches that run out from the land afford magnificent fishing-grounds, and their toil was evidently not in vain. Others, more venturesome, strike out on the smooth water in the roughest kind of boats—the trunk of a tree scooped out, with outriggers on both sides, to which are attached spars balancing their craft. These contrivances do not lend themselves to the use of oars, and are usually propelled by a man in the stern with a long pole, which he pushes against the shallow sea-bottom. A more ambitious boat for coasting purposes is made out of the trunk of the eccentric baobab tree. These trees rise out of the surrounding brushwood on the shore with a weird and almost ghostly aspect, as if they were dead, their crooked branches standing out in uncouth forms against the sky at night. They are leafless when every other tree is crowded with foliage. But the baobab tree throws out its own leaves in its own time, and clothes itself decently. The two ends of the trunk of these trees are sharpened by the natives. No keel is required, as they are only intended for light draft. The trunk is scooped out so as to hold four or sometimes six people. Two constitute the ordinary crew, and with long poles as propellers they go a fishing. The water is exquisitely clear, with nothing but the merest ripple from the wind on its surface. The Government boat in which we travelled was, however, well built, and we had four capable negroes at the oars. We looked over the sides to the rocky bottom below us. The little caverns of white and red coral were peopled with sea anemones and sponges. Thousands of fish floated undisturbed. Sometimes the natives club together and throw out large nets with corks and leads, with which they intercept the larger fish as the tide ebbs or flows; at other times shoals of fish take fright, and hundreds of them splash the surface, and, springing into the air, fly away to the right hand and the left as we intrude on their solitude. Here and there grotesque coral rocks rise above the surface, shaped like mushrooms, the splash of the tide wearing away the lower part of the rock and leaving the top covered with a mass of brushwood which forms a home for the birds. The Magila Hills, and other mountains on the African mainland, are seen as we coast along these Pemba lagoons.

As we approached Weti, our four boatmen were eagerly expecting Ramadan (the hot month), every day of which the devout Muslim keeps as a fast. Very beautiful was the crescent of the new moon as it appeared at sundown. Before we could see it, the faint streak of curved white light was detected by our boatmen. They bowed and pronounced some Arabic words in a kind of chant, and Ramadan was ushered in. The Mohammedan day commences at sunset. In another moment the booming of the guns from the shore corroborated the observation of the boatmen; the great Mohammedan fast had begun. The fast is religiously observed during the day, but at sunset the kettledrums sound, choruses are sung, processions shout through the streets, and there is much feasting.

Excellent fish was purchased from the boats as we passed, and the negroes thoroughly understood the right price to ask for the fish they had caught. Their Arab masters, to whom the fish or the money must be handed over, had taught them their lesson. What the negroes eat in the way of fish is shell-fish and dried shark! Outside a native village on the plantations are often seen heaps of sea-shells that have accumulated for years; such heaps of shells would be a paradise for English children from which to select decorations for their mantel-pieces at home. The dhows come to shore loaded with dried shark. Unhappy is the Englishman who tarries in the precincts of a newly landed cargo. The smell is repulsive. But the negroes rapidly congregate, and a brisk trade runs on. The fish is cut up into long strips; these are tied together, and the successful purchasers carry them away on their heads and under their arms with delight.

The little islands that fringe the western shores of Zanzibar and Pemba form lovely retreats. Chango, or Prison Island, immediately faces the city of Zanzibar. This island is placed under the care of Captain Agnew, the port officer of the city. He kindly ran us across to it in his boat in thirty-five minutes. It has a beautiful sandy beach, on which we picked up red coral, tropical shells, and sponge. The tall aloes and cactus, the papaw trees, and the fragrant frangi-pani abound. Indiarubber grows here readily as elsewhere. The island is all coral, and full of holes, quarries, and caves. Down in these quarries, lower than the surface of the island, the negroes and half-castes build their huts, plant their bananas, and keep their goats, sheltered from the winds. There are two Government bungalows for the use of officials as sanatoriums. There is also a model prison, which at present lies empty. Mesale is a picturesque island opposite Chaki-Chaki, off Pemba. To the north of Mesale lies Uvinje, which is occasionally visited by the English men-of-war. Other islands are valued by the Arabs as the prolific home of guinea-fowl and wild birds. Fundu is a long island frequented by the Arabs, on which we found a considerable population, who spend their time in fishing and in cultivation. It is sometimes regarded as a health resort. Hamoud-bin-Abdullah, a leading Arab of Nynnyennyeni, whose shamba we visited near Weti, escorted us to Fundu. The islanders gave us a courteous welcome; they were grouped together under a baobab tree on the shore, mending their nets. A charpoy under a wide-spreading mango was our resting-place. Our "boys" fed on the cassava which they gathered and roasted in a brushwood fire. The cassava is a shrub with knotty stems, growing to a height of from five to eight feet, and the roots swell into large tubers of a yellowish colour. An acre of cassava yields more nutritive matter than six acres of wheat; it is therefore a very popular food for the common people, and is abundantly cultivated.* It is planted on well-drained soil on the hill slopes, as the roots soon decay if water-logged. It thrives best in the neighbourhood of the sea. In planting, the full-grown woody stems are cut in pieces four to six inches long, and these are placed in rows in a slanting position in ground which has been prepared with a hoe, and they soon strike root. The tuberous root is easily roasted, and answers the purpose of our potato as an article of diet. It is also,

* Nichols' "Tropical Agriculture."

GATHERING CLOVES.

when dried, made into meal for bread and cakes, or manufactured into starch and tapioca. On the island of Fundu there are very ancient trees with Arabic inscriptions. Cotton grows freely. We gathered a handful of fragrant orchids, which luxuriate on trees in the swamps.

The heavy rainfall of the islands is largely affected by the monsoons. Lying five degrees south of the equator, the highest temperature is in January, February, and March, and the lowest in July, August, and September. To Europeans the equable temperature is very striking. Throughout the whole year it does not usually vary more than ten or twelve degrees, ranging from 78° to 88°, seldom registering over 90°. The first three months and the last three months in the year the prevailing winds are from the east and north-east. In these months the islands are under the influence of the north-east monsoon, which almost daily brings fresh breezes. In April, May, and June comes the heavy south-west monsoon, which brings abundance of rain, amounting to about 15 inches in April.

The exports from Zanzibar and Pemba consist chiefly of cloves and copra. The export trade in indiarubber, ivory, tortoise-shell, gum, and chillies is also considerable. The clove is the staple commodity, and pays a duty of 25 per cent. in kind to the Zanzibar Government. The export of cloves for the last five years has been 74,602,000lbs., giving an average annual export of 14,920,458lbs.; the output in the year 1896 was 12,490,835lbs., which was less than for some years past. Five-sevenths of the entire clove crop comes from Pemba, the smaller of the two islands, so that the commercial prosperity of Pemba largely depends on this culture. The people, however, show great carelessness in the cultivation of the plantations, in picking the trees, in drying the cloves for market, in the packing, and in the shipment. The energy of free labour may, we hope, ultimately alter this. Scarcely less important is the export of copra, the white meat of the cocoanut, 12,927,208lbs. being sent out in 1896, valued at £64,802. This was considerably in excess of previous years. It is packed in sacks, and sent for the most part to Marseilles, being largely used in the manufacture of sweetmeats and biscuit confectionery. Copra has the great advantage of paying no export duty. Of chillies, 579,285lbs. were exported in 1896. Some conception may thus be gained of the main natural products of the islands available for commerce. But such statistics take no account of the abundant produce, such as bananas, rice, and cassava, which form the ordinary food-stuffs of the bulk of the inhabitants.

By far the largest annual imports into the islands of Zanzibar and Pemba are from India. This is, of course, partly the result of easy communication with Bombay; but the fact reflects great credit on the Hindu and Parsi merchants. German East Africa stands next on the list for imports. Germany also supplies the islands with far more piece-goods than any other country, the latest Blue-book on the subject stating that for the "kangas," which form the principal dress of Swahili women, " Germany practically holds the monopoly." This monopoly is not the result of tariff, but of open competition in meeting the requirements of the market. The same remark applies to cotton sheetings. Those which sell most freely in Zanzibar are all of American manufacture, and are preferred before English sheetings. "The cloths imported from America," the Government Blue-book states, "are of a superior quality to those of the same price sent from

NATURAL RESOURCES.

Manchester." These facts have been submitted by our Government to the Manchester Chamber of Commerce, and therefore need not be dilated upon here. After India and German East Africa come the imports from Great Britain, which were larger in 1896 than in 1895.

There is, as yet, no direct line of steamers running from England either to Zanzibar or to the ports on the East African coast. There is an excellent French line from Marseilles, also a German line from Europe to Zanzibar.

LIFE ON THE SHAMBA.

CHAPTER III.

SLAVERY AS IT WAS.

"God has created no man despicable."—*Swahili Proverb*.

THE Koran often speaks kindly of the slave. An Arab Sheikh on Pemba liberated a number of his slaves, and on being asked why he had done so, promptly quoted the Koran and replied, "Because it is well-pleasing to God." There are kind masters as well as cruel, and it is not to the interest of the master to illtreat or starve his slave, any more than it is his interest to illtreat a horse or a mule. It is a fallacy to charge the Arabs with all the enormities of slave-raiding and slave-trading in Africa. Slavery existed long before the Arab went to Africa. It is ingrained in the social life of the dark continent. It was found in Madagascar and Mozambique, in South Africa and in West Africa, outside Arab influence; and English merchants themselves were for generations guilty of fostering the slave trade between West Africa and America.

Dr. Heanley says: "England may have forgotten, but the African too well remembers, the English pirates, who came to prey upon the Portuguese commerce, and left behind them no honourable memory of Englishmen or Christians." Thousands of Africans have died in miserable slavery in order that Englishmen might make fortunes. Captain Lugard with equal emphasis says: "Our horror-stricken outcries in Europe against the unspeakable atrocities of the 'Arab' slave-raider ill become us when we look back at the history of the past, and recall the fact that for two and a-half centuries we ourselves stained our hands with this traffic, and pocketed the gold which was the price of human blood. We have thus a duty of expiation to perform towards the African." Let us therefore honestly consider the debt we owe to Africa.

Many intelligent people seem to think that slavery as a domestic institution of the people is not in itself bad for the negro, but that it is the slave-raiding and slave trade that are cruel. All three hang together; but our present consideration is the actual condition of slavery in itself. The moral degradation of slavery is one of its worst features and a gigantic wrong. The terrible violation and abrogation of home life and of the sanctities of home purity are the unutterable condemnation of slavery everywhere. Probably no one is able to speak to this point with more emphasis than Miss Thackeray, of Mbweni. It was delightful to listen to her as her coloured protégés gathered round her. Many of the freed girls who have been handed to her by the Government are happily married. Referring to these married girls, she said with enthusiastic joy, "I have now ninety-one grandchildren and one great-grandchild." Her life is consecrated to this work among negro women and girls in Zanzibar. Speaking from observation, she says: "I have seen so much of slavery in connection with these children that I know the horrors of it too well not to long for immediate emancipation. It is the *deterioration of character* incident to slavery that is the worst feature of all." Slavery hardens the heart of the master and mistress, and deadens the moral sensibilities of the victim. Man as man was held in little estimation when he could be bought or sold for a few rupees. The Arab would often give six times as much for a donkey as for a slave.

We heard, both in Zanzibar and in Pemba, narratives of awful cruelty inflicted on the slaves by the Arabs. Cruelty is by no means confined to the horrors of the slave-raiding on peaceful villages in the interior of Africa, and the fearful slave caravans. Where man has absolute power over his fellow-man cruelties will occur. But it is unprofitable now to recapitulate horrors, when the Government has, we trust, by its recent action prevented their recurrence. One of the most cruel slaveholders of Pemba is incarcerated in prison in Zanzibar. No more runaway slaves are to be delivered up by *askaris* to their masters. One of the dark features of slavery in Zanzibar and Pemba has been the way in which the Arabs discountenance the negroes from rearing children. Captain Lugard, in speaking from detailed knowledge of our East Africa Protectorate, says: " It is a known fact that slaves do not increase naturally to any appreciable extent." It is asserted by those best able to give evidence that there is a great deal of infanticide. There is on the part of many Arabs a fearful disregard of moral restraint, and under such a system as slavery it is no wonder that the negroes themselves become immoral.

The hopeless servility of the African slave, his docility and acquiescence, often his apparent contentment in his subject condition, is a strange contrast to the love of independence in the Teutonic races. Through the island of Pemba the common salutation of a slave as he passes an Arab is, "*Shi-ka-moo*" ("I place my head under your feet"), a term never used except by a slave; while the self-righteous Arab replies, "Well, in the name of God." Thus the whole system is demoralising and degrading, and the sooner it is extinct the better.

Running slaves in from the mainland had for the most part ceased when we were in Zanzibar and Pemba. Those that were brought in were mostly smuggled in small boats and not in dhows. While we were in Chaki-Chaki two poor fellows who had been stolen from the German sphere of influence were thus landed. The men that kidnapped them had used them as ordinary porters, and for a few pice got them to bring some packages to their boat. The negroes had already made some forty or fifty rupees as porters on the coast, and did as they were bid. Once in the boat, they were seized, one of them who resisted was severely wounded on the head with a weapon, so as to render him helpless, and they were then brought across and run into one of the little creeks on Pemba, to be sold as slaves. The Consul heard of the incident, rescued the two men and took them to the Consulate to keep them from further harm, returning them on the first opportunity to their home on the mainland. But although *askaris* were at once sent to find the culprits who had done the kidnapping, they were in safe hiding, and, if needs be, could well afford to bribe the *askaris*.

Before the abolition of the legal status of slavery the Government officials were accustomed to issue emancipation papers to slaves that were illtreated. The custom in Pemba respecting these " papers of freedom " was peculiar. If a slave belonging to a member of any Arab tribe was set free, he received a paper from the authorities declaring his freedom, and henceforth was described as a freeman of that tribe. Thus, if our friend Sulieman bin Said or his son for any cause set a slave free, he was henceforth called and called himself " the freeman of Sulieman-bin-Said." Thus also the slaves whom the Vice-Consul set free for acts of injustice or cruelty inflicted by their master were henceforth known as the " freemen of the Consul." One man whom the Vice-Consul had thus set free lost his emancipation paper, and was in great terror lest his old master should catch him and again make him a slave. They usually carry their papers in their girdle or in their cap. The man had been sleeping with another negro, who had stolen his emancipation paper for his own use. Vice-Consul O'Sullivan gave the man a fresh paper in order to ensure his safety. The incident proves that the negroes value freedom.

While we were staying at Tunduana an Arab deputation came from the north of the island. Our friend Herbert Lister asked the northern Arab sheikh, " What will happen if the Government sets the slaves free ?" The Arab considered the matter, and then answered, " The same thing will happen that occurred when the Government purchased this estate, and called together all the people living on it and set them all free. There will be no disturbance. Some of the people will, as they did then, choose to move off elsewhere, either to their former homes or to the towns. But a large number, when set free, will willingly remain to work on the same estate where they have been previously located, and will not want to move off. But," added the Arab, " if the Government sets all our slaves free which we have held so long in accordance with the law under which we Mohammedans live, surely we may expect them to pay us for the value of the slaves they take from us." This probably represented the common feeling on the subject among the Arabs previous to the decree abolishing the legal status of slavery. There were no indications that they would rebel, but they looked for what they considered fair treatment. What took place at Tunduaua on the purchase of the property by the Government was that General Sir William Lloyd Mathews and Mr. C. W. Strickland, the collector of revenue, gathered together at the bungalow all the people living on the estate. They gave something like two rupees to the men and one rupee to the women and children as backsheesh, as they assembled to the *shauri* or palaver. They were then informed that the Government had taken over the shamba, and that henceforth all the people living on it were free. They could either go or stay, and were told that if they were willing to stay huts would be given them for their use, and allotments of land for the cultivation of their m'hogo, maize, and pulse, and that those who remained to work on the estate should have regular wages. The people then divided. About half of them, out of some 150, ultimately remained.

Slavery is very wasteful. The men just fulfil their appointed task without energy and without hope. The clove harvest is generally negligently gathered, and there is great carelessness in the drying and packing of the cloves for market. Failure is written on the old system, and even from a commercial point of view it is quite time a better plan was adopted.

The slave girls are the water-carriers of East Africa. In Zanzibar and Pemba they were daily seen going to and from the wells. They walk erect, balancing their load on their heads, and they have become so accustomed to this erect bearing that they maintain it everywhere, and you never see a slave girl with a slovenly stooping gait such as is common among the working classes in England. Day after day in Chaki-Chaki we watched the slave girls

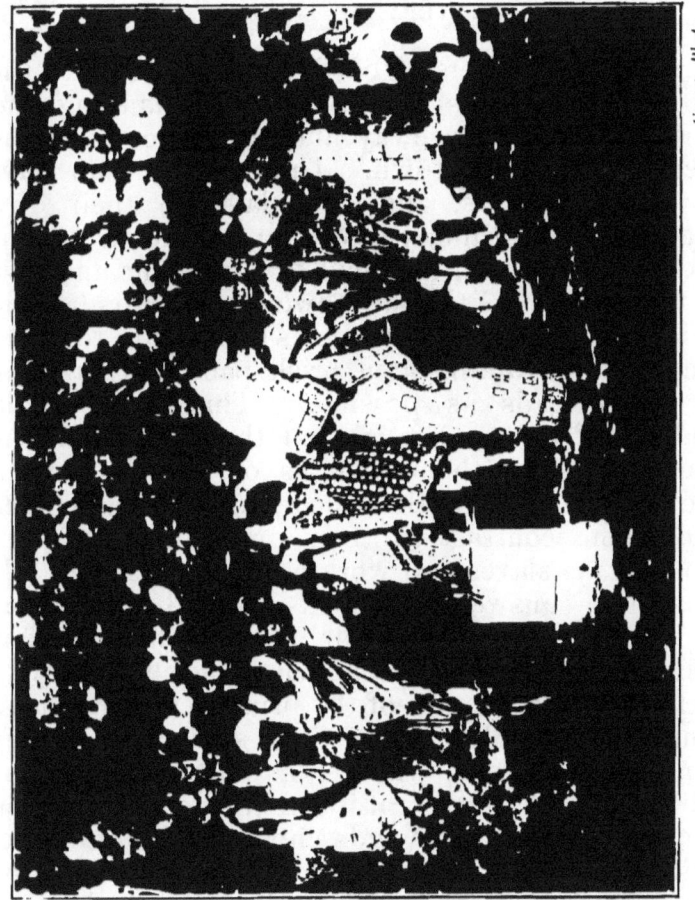

SLAVE GIRLS, WATER-CARRIERS OF ZANZIBAR.

carrying the baskets of earth on their heads at the Government works in improving the landing and making a new causeway and staircase from the creek up into the town. They worked four days for their masters, and two days on their own account. On ordinary days they would earn about sixteen pice, which they had to take home and give to their masters. On their own days (Thursday and Friday) they earned as much as twenty-five to thirty pice a day, walking at a brisk pace and carrying as many loads as possible. Thus they would make half as much again on the days when the wages came to themselves as on the days when the money went to their masters. The difference shows the contrast in their own minds between working as slaves and working for themselves. It is also an answer to the oft-repeated question as to whether the negro will work if offered a fair wage, and as to whether he has sufficient energy of character to make use of the privileges of freedom. One of the peculiarities of these slaves is that they sing as they work, whether as porters or as day labourers. In Zanzibar it is common to hear the men singing together some rude chorus of infinite repetition in Swahili as they carry their loads from the beach to the Custom-house, or from the go-down to the dhow. The heavier their loads the more they seem to sing. The girls in Chaki-Chaki with their baskets of earth were singing a Swahili song gaily as they passed to and fro. The gentleman who was with me called my attention to their song, remarking that it was their own impromptu, and that they improvised it as they ran along. It was a chorus respecting Ali-bin-Abdulla, of Pemba, who in March, 1896, was convicted of cruelty to a slave and sentenced to seven years' imprisonment. The chorus ran after this fashion :—

> "We used to cry for mercy,
> But for us there was no mercy;
> Now he that had no mercy on us
> Is shut up in the European's
> Stone house in Zanzibar."

These girls were still slaves, but the masters had learned that they could not abuse them with impunity, and the girls themselves were lifting up their heads, as though conscious that the day of their redemption was drawing nigh. It is thus manifest that before the recent decree of the Sultan a marked change for the better had taken place among the people. But slavery lies too deeply ingrained in the heart of the people to be suddenly exorcised by any edict, however well intentioned.

A woman came into the Court shortly before our arrival and accused a man of having unjustly enslaved her. Evidence was produced and the woman was liberated. The man was fined forty rupees for his crime, and twenty rupees were handed to the woman as compensation for the wrong that she had suffered. She was asked shortly afterwards what she was going to do with the twenty rupees. She at once answered, "I shall buy a slave with it." This was of course illegal, but in Africa illegal things are done with impunity.

In crossing from Pemba to Zanzibar we had on board the *Barawa* three negroes who had been illegally brought from the mainland, and who had been hidden away as slaves in Pemba. They had been discovered and emancipated by the Government. The Consul promised to get them work and regular wages either in Pemba or in Zanzibar. They replied that they were willing to work for wages for a time, but they wanted to return to their home on the mainland. The Government accordingly gave them a free passage. This is one of the many difficult problems that have to be dealt with on emancipation. Both islands urgently need more labour. They can ill afford to lose what they now have. There is great danger that in many cases, on returning to the mainland, they may be kidnapped and again made slaves. But they voluntarily run this risk in the uncertain hope of reaching again their own people. A Christian native, who was living far from his old home in East Africa, used to go wistfully to a hill-top, and look out across the landscape to Bondé, calling pathetically, " Bondé, Bondé, Bondé !" This natural love for home is something we cannot fail to respect, although it might be much more convenient to us for the natives to remain on the plantations where they are located. Freedom involves the option of return to their fatherland ; and though we may call it sentiment, the love of country that burns strongly in the Englishman is also present in the African. H. M. Stanley says, after observation of native character, " I was much comforted in observing that they were as ready to be influenced by passions, by loves and hates, as I was myself; that the keenest observation failed to detect any great difference between their nature and my own."* On the *Barawa* I had an admirable illustration of this brotherhood. Two miles out of Zanzibar we slackened speed to take on board a little black lad, who was named Mufta. He had been rescued from a cruel slavery by Mr. Herbert Lister, who was on board our ship, and the boy only felt safe in his presence. Mr. Lister had been for some hours in Zanzibar, and the boy dreaded the thought of being recaptured by his old master. Across the sea went the cry from our steamer to the ship lying at anchor, " Mufta ! Mufta !" and over the side of the other vessel the boy

---

* "How I found Livingstone," page 16.

appeared, clambering in a hurry into the boat, and was quickly on board. He became very familiar afterwards. He was jet black, sleek and shining. With a few pice he bought himself a yellow tunic with a crimson girdle, and a white cap. He would lie at night on the mat outside his master's bedroom door, or curled like a hedgehog in a corner; but wherever he was, it was sunshine and security to him to be near Mr. Lister.

Those who know what slavery is know how to appreciate freedom. A man came a long distance into Chaki-Chaki from a country shamba. He had heavy irons on his ankles, but had made a sort of cotton padding under the fetters to save injuring the bone. Attaching a piece of tough bark fibre to the iron that fastened his legs together, he lifted the weight of the fetters off his feet by holding the fibre firmly in his hand. Then by a series of little jumps along the foot-track he succeeded in the night in making his way to Chaki-Chaki prison, where he knew he was safe from his master. A score of men did their best to loosen the fetters, but without success. In the morning he stood before us with a piteous look, as if imploring help, and the authorities concluded to emancipate him. But how could he be emancipated with such fetters on? The man looked hopeless, but the order was given, "Give the man a file, and let him file himself free." The filing was a slow process, but the result was freedom. Until men are roused to energy to secure their own freedom, the liberty others obtain for them fails to raise them up. It is therefore necessary to consider a somewhat wider question, and that is, the native as a social factor for the building up of a brighter future for Africa.

CHAPTER IV.

THE AFRICAN AS A SOCIAL FACTOR.

"It is folly to slaughter a goat for the sake of a chop."—*Swahili Proverb.*

THE blight of slavery has rested on the islands so long that it is not quickly dispelled. The native of East Africa, whether on the mainland or in Zanzibar, is a long way behind his more civilised cousin in America. He has neither the resourcefulness of the American negro, nor the ambition. He has not, as yet, the necessary backbone of character, and he needs the presence of the white man to lead him forward. One of the marvels in America was that the negro cordially accepted the white man's religion, and adopted Christianity more thoroughly than the negro in East Africa adopted Mohammedanism. He imitates the white man's ways in either case.

In the negro settlements in the "black belt" of the Southern States, one is everywhere struck with the multitude of children. A number of little curly heads crowd round the door when the white visitor appears in Carolina or Tennessee, in Alabama or Arkansas. Not so in Pemba. Yet the negro in East Africa has this great advantage, that he outnumbers all other elements in the population. He constitutes two-thirds of the population in Zanzibar and Pemba; and with freedom children will come, and children's children. Districts on the mainland that have been desolated and swept of the entire population by the slave-raiders rapidly refill

NATIVE BOYS AND GIRLS AND HUTS, ZANZIBAR.

when confidence is re-established, and this in itself proves the immense capacity of the race to recoup itself in the tropics when fairly treated. The white man cannot colonise Equatoria to any large extent, except on the elevated tableland. But the European is requisite in the administration of an advancing civilisation. Left to himself, the African is apathetic and indolent. He loves his native land and his tropical environment, and it does better for him than for the European. Downtrodden, he is like a strong ass couching between two burdens. He saw that rest was good and the land that it was pleasant, and bowed his shoulder to bear, and became a servant under task-work. When the English rajah steps in and endeavours to raise the negro to higher things, he will often side with his Mohammedan master rather than with the European. Even when he is set free by an enlightened maternal Government, he will remember, like the Israelites, the good times in bondage, "when we sat by the fleshpots, and when we did eat bread to the full." But this is no argument against emancipation.

The *Daily Telegraph* speaks of the "inborn cheerfulness of disposition" of the African, and it has served him in good stead. He sings and dances to his heart's content, not because he is a slave, but by some recuperative force that puzzles the European. Nature abounds with charming compensations. Whilst we were quietly reading or writing in our upstairs rooms in the evening, our "boys," by the light of an oil lamp, would dance by the hour to some rude kettle-drum in the verandah below, and the silhouettes reflected on the opposite wall were diverting. On a Sabbath they dress in any of the colours of the rainbow that are accessible to them, and look far more picturesque than any black-coated Englishman. Nothing save evil custom can account for the ugly tattooing of the faces of the women in some tribes. Still more outrageous are the decorations of the girls in the streets of Mombasa, by the insertion of brass discs in the lobe of the ears, and the disfigurement of the protruding and distended lip by the flat disc thrust into it. But the dark colour of the negro skin is much more appropriate in the tropics than the pale and sallow complexion of the European.

Mercy is not a marked characteristic of the African. We met a group of merry, curly-headed girls in a narrow foot-track in the country. Hanging by a thread from their fingers, and tied by the legs, were the most brilliant little birds, their coloured feathers sparkling in the sunshine. We talked to the children, but, though slaves themselves, it did not enter their minds that the captive birds had any claim for kindness.

Few men have had more experience of the Swahilis of East Africa, under a great variety of circumstances, than Captain Lugard. He describes them as the product of the system of slave-buying and slave-catching which the Muscat Arabs have carried on for two centuries. Boy slaves brought from the interior, and belonging to various tribes from the Zambesi in the south to the Tana in the north, grew up in their households, took their ideas from them, and too often their vices. There was also a percentage of half-breeds, the offspring of Arabs by slave concubines. A language grew up, founded on the various tongues spoken by these captured slaves, who usually belonged to the great negro stock, with woolly heads and flat noses; and these races, from their physical development and strength, furnished the best type for the slaver's purpose. Moreover, their childlike adaptability, and their eager imitation of their masters, made them pre-eminently useful as slaves. Taught from their childhood to carry heavy burdens, they bore on their heads the goods necessary for barter in the interior, and the other paraphernalia of their masters, in loads of from 60lbs. to 80lbs. Captain Lugard thus sums up the capacity of these Swahilis, or coast-men :—" I know no such typical raw material in the world ; you can mould them as you will. Some of them have even the making of heroes in them, as many instances vivid in my memory attest ; some of them have qualifications for all that is the reverse ; most of them are singularly easily trained to be willing workers, most patient of hardships, plucky, ready to expose their lives, adaptable to routine and discipline, however novel and unwelcome. The rapidity with which these men had accustomed themselves to the white man's routine and discipline struck me as a singular phenomenon."*

We can bear witness to the truth of this description. Their perseverance in working at the oars hour after hour, without a murmur and with many a chorus and pleasant joke, called forth our admiration. As carriers of burdens they are marvellous people, and do it with a willing-heartedness and cheerfulness that is an example to Teutons. They carry the heavy European across creeks and muddy shoals at low tide without hesitation. Landing is a common difficulty where there are no harbours, no quay-sides, no landing-places. The boat is run smartly aground, and then through the shallow water the native boatmen wade with their passengers clinging round their necks, one passenger between two boatmen. Many an amusing episode occurs. The European looks undignified, but is safely landed.

* Captain Lugard, " Rise of our East African Empire," vol. i., page 238.

Lieutenant C. S. Smith, late Vice-Consul at Zanzibar, after long experience, says "he does not think the negroes are incorrigibly lazy, and considers that they are more amenable to discipline than white men under similar circumstances." Another reliable and cautious witness to the character and capacity of the negro is J. Scott Keltie. He justly says:—"For the future development of Africa it is with the negroes and Bantus we shall have mainly to reckon. Without labour we cannot develop the continent; and if we cannot get the native to work, what is to become of Africa? We are often told that the negro is a lazy being, who never will be trained to habits of industry. But as a universal statement, facts belie that assertion. He does work, and that often with great steadiness and regularity. On some of the plantations of the Germans, inland from Zanzibar, the people came quite willingly to work, induced to do so by the wages offered. At the same time it must be admitted that voluntary hard work is not congenial to a people who for ages have been accustomed to do no more than they were forced to do. It should be quite possible, by judicious treatment, to lead the natives on to industrious habits; but we must not expect, in this and other matters, to force them in a generation or two up to a stage which it has taken us 2,000 years to reach."* J. Scott Keltie sums up the evidence on this subject in Africa by two axioms: Firstly, "that if the resources of the continent are to be developed, it must be by the help of the natives"; and secondly, "It must be done by the natives under the guidance of others who have reached a higher stage of civilisation than they have." "But in Africa we have undoubted instances of the natives being induced to undertake

* J. Scott Keltie, "The Partition of Africa," page 486.

CUSTOM-HOUSE, CHAKI-CHAKI, PEMBA.

hard work for wages, of their own free will."* He cites the work of the Scotch missionaries at Blantyre: " Thousands of acres are under coffee plantations, and thousands more have been taken up by English planters to be brought under cultivation. The natives, who a few years ago lived in the wildest savagery, come hundreds of miles voluntarily to beg for work in these plantations. Many of them have been trained to various trades. The church, designed by a Scotch missionary, was built entirely by the natives with free labour. He and his colleagues taught the natives to make bricks, burn lime, and hew timber. All the materials were found on the spot, except glass, internal fittings, and some portion of the roofing. They were put together, brick upon brick, by the natives themselves, free labourers under white superintendence. Here there is not the least suspicion of compulsion, and the result is wonderful. We may banish the unfounded idea that the African native can never be trained to labour."†

In forming an estimate of the native as a factor in the regeneration of Africa, it is essential that we should also recognise the weak points we have to deal with. The late Bishop Steere, of Zanzibar, after many years' experience, said :—" The races of tropical Africa, being among the lowest of the human family, need very special self-sacrifice as the instrument of their elevation. Among their most prominent defects are the love of capricious self-indulgence, working itself out in idleness, gluttony, drunkenness, and uncleanness ; whilst slavery, the worst scourge of these races, helps to make labour distasteful, and therefore progress impossible."‡

Henry M. Stanley, speaking of the slaves of

---

* J. Scott Keltie, " The Partition of Africa," page 506.   † *Ibid.*, page 508.
‡ " Memoir of Bishop Steere," page 333.

Zanzibar, says:—"Outside the city they may be seen carrying huge loads on their heads, as happy as possible, not because they are kindly treated or that their work is light, but because it is their nature to be gay and light-hearted."*

One more witness claims consideration, James Stewart, of Lovedale. "The African," he says, "is deserving of better treatment. He has his faults, as men of all races have, but he shows a docility, affection, and loyalty to the white man when he is thoroughly trusted, scarcely shown by any other race at the same social level. His trust in the white man's rectitude and power is absolute, until he is rudely undeceived, as he has been ten thousand times, by some startling disclosure of the absence of that rectitude." Again he says:—"The population of Africa will steadily increase, now that the slave trade is doomed, and all civilised nations have, formally at least, washed their hands of that great iniquity. In the African continent, wherever its people can enjoy a few years of peace, its desert places again become filled with life. The villages raided and burned by slavers, and out of which a few terror-stricken fugitives escaped with nothing but bare life, are again rebuilt; the fields are cultivated, and the village becomes noisy with the life and play of children."†

There is a sort of easy-going indolence among these people that is difficult to dispel. "Raw" slaves that have been recently brought down from the interior have much more of the spirit of resistance in them. When recently captured they are often severely wounded, and are fettered in order to make them submissive.

The people of the East Coast of Africa and of

* H. M. Stanley, "How I found Livingstone," page 16.
† James Stewart, "Lovedale, South Africa," page 54.

the Equatorial Provinces are not, for the most part, strictly speaking, negroes. They are of various tribes, and many of them may be roughly classified as of the Bantu race.

Everything points to the establishment of one leading axiom in all African affairs, and that is, that *the future development of tropical Africa must be the work of the natives themselves under enlightened European supervision.* The Congo Free State tried the experiment of importing Chinese coolies in the place of native labour. Within a few months nearly 500 died, and most of the others decamped. Africa absolutely needs the administrative faculty that Englishmen and Germans can so ably supply. Leadership pertains to the European, but Africa is for the Africans, and it is by the development of the African that it can alone be developed. The native African is the plastic material essential to success. It is but a repetition and reiteration of the doctrine of the solidarity of mankind. "The eye cannot say to the hand, I have no need of thee: or the head to the feet, I have no need of you. Nay, much rather, those members of the body which seem to be more feeble are necessary. Whether one member suffereth, all the members suffer with it; or one member is honoured, all the members rejoice with it." There would therefore appear to be a good providence in the establishment of the European Protectorates on the dark continent, and the movement of the last fifteen years in this direction promises to be the succour and the salvation of the African race and the replenishment of Africa.

CHAPTER V.

THE ARAB AS A SOCIAL FACTOR.

" He that gives full play to his desires will drown in shallow water."
Swahili Proverb.

The presence of the Arab in East Africa is an important factor in any consideration respecting future development. The Arab has displayed a vigour and executive power that must be recognised by any Government. From circumstances inherent to his mode of life, that faculty has fatally degenerated; but many Arabs to-day evidence real administrative ability. A glance at their remarkable history enables us to recognise their ability, however much we may controvert their methods.

In the year 740 A.D., Said, the great-grandson of Ali, the cousin and son-in-law of Mohamed, having been proclaimed Caliph by a schismatic party, was defeated and slain, and his adherents fled to East Africa.* A considerable emigration from Arabia and from Persia followed, owing to religious troubles. Thus in the tenth century a number of towns were established along the coast, and they continued to grow and flourish, attaining considerable strength and prosperity, a number of fugitives from Shiraz emigrating thither. In 1331 an Arab author named Ibn-Batuta describes Mombasa as a considerable city, and the ruins of forts existing there and at other places along the coast show that these strongholds were well built and fortified. The coast settlements appear to have been often independent

* "Government Handbook of British East Africa," page 151.

of each other, and to have traded with the interior. In this way was gradually formed the Zenj Empire, from which we have the name of Zanzibar; and thus was formed the Swahili or coast population, with their African speech, their admixture of Asiatic blood, and their Arab religion. The Portuguese appear to have been the first European power who attempted to dispute possession with these Arab settlers. Vasco da Gama, the great and brave navigator, touched at Mombasa and Malindi in 1498. Mombasa fell into the hands of the Portuguese in 1500. They also seized Lamu, Zanzibar, and Malindi, and by 1528 the East Coast had been conquered, and was retained by Portugal for 150 years. From 1660 to 1698 the Arabs again regained ascendency.

A large part of the East African coast was nominally under the jurisdiction of the Imams of Muscat, though there were constant attempts on the part of local Sultans to establish their independence. The term *Sultan* in East Africa has often a very uncertain sound, and does not necessarily represent supreme power, but rather one who by inheritance or by the power of his own sword has succeeded in obtaining authority. In the year 1698 the Imam of Oman sailed from Muscat, in the Persian Gulf, and conquered Zanzibar, which thenceforth for many years became a dependency of Muscat. The East Coast of Africa gradually fell under his dominion, and the Muscat Arabs settled on the islands along the mainland. They held the coastline for hundreds of miles, and with adventurous courage penetrated into the interior with armed caravans in search of ivory and slaves.* In this development of Arab supremacy they had frequent conflicts with the Portuguese, who had adopted

* Lugard's "East Africa," vol. i., page 239.

the system of occupying positions on the coast without really exercising sovereignty in the interior. Andrade Corvo, the Portuguese historian, gives an amusing description of the way in which the Arabs prevailed over the Portuguese, while sometimes the latter obtained the ascendency. He describes the result. "It was," he says, "one full of woes for our colonies in the East, and particularly in East Africa. The Kaffirs in the south, and the Arabs in the north, attacked our dominions and punished us most cruelly for our frankness. At times victors, and at others beaten on all sides, we dragged out a sad existence."* In the year 1804 the Sultan Seyyid Saïd ascended the throne, and for fifty-two years this monarch ruled with power, firmly establishing the Sultanate of Zanzibar as an offshoot of Oman, and controlling the coast. On the change of dynasty in Oman, which took place on the accession of Al-bin-Saidi, several subordinate Governors on the East Coast refused allegiance. After constant friction, the Sultanate of Zanzibar, however, became an independent and dominant power, and was recognised as such by Great Britain. Seyyid Saïd made himself master of Patta, Brava, Lamu, Zanzibar, Pemba, and Kilwa, and threatened to attack Mombasa, where the aged Suliman Ben Ali, as representing the Governor under the older rulers of Oman, was in power. Suliman appealed to Captain Owen,† the English squadron at that time being engaged in surveying the coast, and in 1824 Great Britain took under its protection Mombasa, Pemba, and all the coast between Malindi and Pangani. At the end of four years our Government abandoned this concession, and left East Africa in the hands of the Sultans for nearly sixty years. Seyyid Saïd built

* Keltie's "Partition of Africa," page 56.   † *Ibid.*, page 106.

MARKET-PLACE, CHAKI-CHAKI, PEMBA.

T. Burtt, Photo.

his palace at Zanzibar, and established his headquarters there, and in 1841 Captain Hammerton became the first English Consul to Zanzibar. On the death of the venerable Sultan Seyyid Saïd at the Seychelles, in 1856, there was a hot conflict for the succession between his lineal descendants, but an amicable partition of his dominions was effected, and was ultimately confirmed by the Government of India in 1861, under Lord Canning, Seyyid Thwain obtaining the Sultanate of Oman, in the Persian Gulf, while the Sultanate of Zanzibar fell to the lot of his brother, Seyyid Majid. The struggles of Mombasa for independence continued, but Seyyid Majid prevailed and established the supremacy of the Sultanate of Zanzibar over the whole coast from Cape Delgado to Magadisho. He reigned for some fourteen years, and on his death was succeeded, on the 7th October, 1870, by Seyyid Burghash, the brother of Majid. Burghash was one of the ablest Arab administrators that ever governed Zanzibar. The impress of his masterful spirit is still found in the island. For eighteen years he maintained the ascendency of the Arab power with vigour. While France and England were competing for spheres of influence, the strong hand of Germany ultimately appeared upon the scene. Burghash was strong, but there was one man in Zanzibar who was stronger, that was Sir John Kirk. Quietly but firmly Sir John maintained English influence. He understood Oriental life. He kept steadily in view the advancement of sound government. Persistently, yet wisely, he resisted the slave trade, which had assumed considerable proportions, and at the same time did a great deal to introduce into the islands new products for culture. Some of the plants which now seem indigenous in Zanzibar were thus introduced. Hence, while firmly adhering to what he regarded as the true line of progress, it was manifest to the Sultan and to the people at large that Sir John Kirk had at heart the welfare of the country. Sir John's career in Zanzibar runs from 1866 to 1887. In 1872 Sir Bartle Frere had been appointed Special Envoy to the Sultans of Zanzibar and Muscat, to induce them both to sign a treaty rendering the export of slaves from Africa illegal. Burghash obstinately objected, for the slave trade was a source of large revenue at that time to the Arabs, many of whom were extensive slave-holders; but through the astute persuasion of Sir John Kirk the Sultan at last signed the treaty on the 5th June, 1873. In 1875 the Sultan visited England, and was cordially welcomed, in person, by the Queen. He died in 1888, and was succeeded on the 26th March by his brother, Seyyid Khalifa, who died in 1890, and was followed by another brother, Seyyid Ali. He also died, about thirty-eight years of age, on the 5th March, 1893, and then arose the vexed question of the succession.

The Sultans who had rapidly succeeded each other had all been brothers, and Ali was the youngest of the numerous sons of the patriarch Seyyid Saïd, who had died in 1856. There was still a surviving brother of the same family, Abdul Aziz-bin-Saïd. Two of the sons of Seyyid Saïd, Thwain and Turki, had now been Sultans of Muscat, and four others of them had been in succession Sultans of Zanzibar. Abdul Aziz, the surviving brother, was residing in India, and considered himself to be the legitimate successor. Sir Bartle Frere asked Abdul Aziz what was the law of succession in Muscat, and Abdul, glancing significantly at the dagger in his girdle, and moving the fingers of his right hand as if along its blade, replied concisely,

"The law of the keenest edge." When Thwain (the immediate successor of Seyyid Saïd to the throne of Oman) was murdered in 1866 by his own son, his son's dagger fell to the ground as he bowed himself in prayer over his father's dead body, and Turki, who succeeded to the throne of Muscat on the death of his brother Thwain, was regarded as a coward because he did not at once seize the dagger as it lay on the ground and bury it in the heart of his nephew who had committed the murder.

Whatever murders or poisonings have taken place in the succession of the Sultans, "the law of the keenest edge" has not always availed, and the English Government refused to allow Abdul Aziz to leave India, instructing the police to prevent him from sailing for Zanzibar; and instead of allowing him to succeed to the throne which his brother Ali's death had rendered vacant in 1893, the British Foreign Office decreed that Hamed-bin-Thwain-bin-Saïd should succeed to the Sultanate of Zanzibar. He was a nephew of Abdul Aziz, and of Burghash, Khalifa, and Ali, and was the son of Seyyid Thwain, the late Sultan of Muscat. Thwain-bin-Saïd, the owner of 30,000 slaves, died unexpectedly at the age of forty, on the 25th August, 1896, and then another dispute sprang up respecting the succession. The accustomed succession among the sons of the venerable Seyyid Saïd had already been departed from by our Government, and Khalid, an elder nephew of Seyyid Saïd, and a son of Burghash, deemed he had as good a right to the Sultanate as any of his cousins, and at once seized the Palace. He was popular among the Arabs, and had already made a formidable effort to obtain the Sultanate previous to the succession of Thwain-bin-Saïd. Many leading Arabs at once gathered round him. He placed 700 armed men in the Palace, and barricaded it against the English. An ultimatum was sent to Khalid by Rear-Admiral Rawson, who called upon him to haul down his flag and surrender by 9 a.m. on the 27th August. Khalid paid no attention either to the Admiral or to the Acting-Agent and Consul, except by preparing for resistance. At 9 a.m. the English ships in the harbour opened fire on the Palace, and in less than forty minutes all opposition was silenced, the Palace was in flames, and Khalid had fled to the German Consulate for refuge. The same day Hamoud was appointed Sultan, and has proved himself amenable to English influence.

On our way to Mbweni, in Zanzibar, we met him with his fourteen wives. He had been resting at a palace on one of his shambas, and was returning with his family to the city. Suddenly a cry was heard, " The Sultan ! The Sultan !" The outriders first appeared, followed by a cavalcade of open carriages. The ladies' faces were not veiled, but each of them wore the *barakoa*. This curious device is a sort of ladies' mask or helmet, reaching down to the upper lip, made of gauze, with an opaque gold band down the centre and across the bottom, leaving the eyes and part of the forehead and the lower lip and chin visible. The veil, thrown back over the head, is of black silk, so as to cover the hair without hiding the face. We were riding with the acting Consul, V. K. Kestell-Cornish, who was taking us to a country station belonging to the Universities' Mission, and the ladies of the Sultan's harem turned towards us as they passed, while our carriage waited at the side of the road. Etiquette ordains that the favourite wives of the Sultan shall have precedence, so that the first carriage contained the ladies in highest favour, and thus on throughout the *cortége*. As one carriage

ZANZIBAR ARABS, LADY WEARING THE BARAKOA.

after another slowly passed we had an opportunity of guaging an Arab's ideal of womanhood. The Sultan followed behind. Recognising Mr. Kestell-Cornish, he immediately bowed to us. The Sultan is a stout, quiet, weary-looking man, appearing as though the life of a private citizen would be preferable to the difficulty and danger of public life. He has, however, bravely roused himself to the responsibilities of his position, and is showing capacity for government, and an honest endeavour to fulfil his important trust.

In some ways the Arabs, who for generations have governed the coast, were an improvement on the Portuguese. They are more *en rapport* with the people they govern, and show a power of assimilation that was singularly absent from the Portuguese. The latter had led a dissolute life, and their attitude was that of traders desiring to make the most of their position and caring little for the welfare of the natives. The Arab, strangely enough, impressed his Muslim faith on the native population. But the climate induced *ennui*, the native was servile, and the Arab ultimately settled down into a genteel indolence that sealed his fate. To-day he has the appearance of a relic of the past, and is effete. He borrows money from the Hindu money-lender, mortgages his property, paying exorbitant interest, and fulfilling the old proverb that the borrower is servant to the lender. The scrupulous Mohammedan objects to usury. To suit his religious predilections, the interest is added to the amount of the loan, and the bond the Arab signs carries what the Americans call a "face value" far above the actual rupees the Hindu hands over. By this means the Muslim conscience is satisfied and the usurer waxes rich. Under such a system it takes but a few years for the Arab gentleman to forfeit his property, and much of the land in Zanzibar and Pemba is loaded down with accumulating mortgages.

Mr. Palgrave justly observes: "Sooner or later, the nation that casts in its lot with Islam is stricken as by a blight; its freshness, its plasticity disappear first, then its reparative and reproductive power disappears, and it petrifies or perishes."* The petrifaction of the Mohammedan of East Africa has set in. The Koran contains many good maxims, but there is in Mohammedanism no regenerating power, and its peoples ultimately fade away. The decay is from within. He is inwardly corrupt and defunct. It is sorrowful that it should be so, for there is much in the Arab character that attracts. He is singularly pleasant and courteous, but unreliable, and, on occasion, terribly cruel. "An Arab cannot dig," they say, and it is a judgment against themselves, convicting them of the fate awaiting them, for it is by the dignity of labour that nations rise. By industry the future is assured, whether to black or white. The Arabs argue that they must have slaves—how else can the work be done? In the long-run the native will work, and win because he works, and the indolent Arab will sink.

Henry M. Stanley gives a portaiture of the Arab as we find him in Zanzibar:—"The Arab never changes. He brought the customs of his forefathers with him when he came to live on this island. He is as much of an Arab here as at Muscat or Bagdad. Wherever he goes to live, he carries with him his harem, his religion, his long robe, his shirt, his slippers, and his dagger. Their various experiences have given their features a certain unmistakable air of self-reliance or of self-sufficiency; there is a calm, resolute, defiant, inde-

* "Memoirs of Bishop Steere," page 120.

pendent air about them, which wins unconsciously one's respect."*

An Englishman on first arrival naturally revolts at seeing "chain-gangs" of natives passing up and down the open streets of Zanzibar, Chaki-Chaki, and Weti. Chain-gangs of women as well as chain-gangs of men are common on both islands. In their chains they work; in chains they march. As I became accustomed to the sorrowful sight, and recognised them as men and women who had been convicted of some crime before the magistrates, it occurred to me, in my simplicity, to inquire, "Why is it always the negroes that sin, and never an Arab in the chain-gang?" Another day I inquired, as I sat in the place of justice, "What is justice here?" And without any hesitation, the answer at once was given, "Whatever the Arab desires is justice here!" Then I knew why the negro only was seen in the chain-gang. In a woman's chain-gang of negroes at Weti we noticed one fine woman standing erect and defiant. It seemed to be the old case of "taming the shrew." Her spirit was not broken. Indignation was marked in her face. The docility of a slave was not in her.

Over and over again I saw the stocks, and the provision for keeping people in the stocks was much more adequate than I had seen in any other part of the world. The stocks easily held half a dozen pairs of guilty feet at once. But they were for black feet. I do not think it occurred to anybody that an Arab could ever be found in the stocks. But the Arabs frequently cheated the Government, cheated their neighbours, and took bribes. The people go to the cadi or to the wali for justice, but if there is no English supervision there is no assurance that justice will be done.

* "How I Found Livingstone," page 11.

When a negro mother and her three children were stolen, the English authorities saw to it that the mother and children were rescued, but the man who gave the information was invited to a feast, and died within two hours of partaking of poisoned food where he had gone as a guest.

If the moral tone of the Arabs is low, their attention to religion is great. Their observance of times of prayer is instructive. Their apparent absorption in prayer is marvellous. The man whose language is foul, and who curses his neighbour, at the appointed hour celebrates his functions of prayer on his knees in the midst of business, whether in his boat or on the sea-shore. The five times of prayer are : immediately after sunset, which is the beginning of a new day ; one hour later ; about four in the morning or at dawn ; at noon ; and about half-past three in the afternoon. Ramadan, when the Mohammedan world fasts for one month from sunrise to sunset, is honoured in all places where Muslims dwell. During that month the men in the towns were quiet in the daytime, attending the mosque, or sitting in their houses reading the Koran aloud to themselves with their curious religious rhythm, gently swaying their bodies to and fro as an accompaniment. At night the drums sounded with shouting and songs in the streets, and the nights were given to revelry. The Arab, with all his faults, is devoutly superstitious.

The Arab is seen at his best in the entertainment of strangers. We carried, through the kindness of General Mathews, a number of introductions to leading sheikhs. With these we visited the best shambas on the island of Pemba. The expressions of welcome that follow on such occasions are excessive. Sitting down with the sheikh Mohamed-bin-Jooma, of Kash-Kash, on his *baraza*, we enjoyed magnificent peeps through the trees of the sparkling sea and the green coral islands beyond. We were regaled with orange sherbet, with dates, coffee, and sweetmeats spread on lordly salvers, while the fragrant otto of roses was sprinkled over our heads in the form of spray by a black slave from the ornamental long-necked *mrashi*. After such preliminaries the topic of conversation usually resolved itself into the labour problem. "What we want is men. We must have labourers to work on the shambas. We have only sixty slaves where we used to have one hundred, and we cannot cultivate our property as we should like. What remedy do you propose? Our men are running away to the mainland. Many go to the German territory. Can we have coolies from India? Can you send us men from Mombasa? We do not care where the men come from so long as we can get our work done. We are willing to give half the produce to the men who gather the cloves if we may have the other half ourselves. No fresh slaves come to the island now, and we do not know what to do." Such was, in effect, the line of conversation in various places we visited. The Arabs recognise that the English Government has done much to secure peace, and they say, "We are at peace, and we have peace one with another." They acknowledge our supremacy, and ask what the Government will do for them in their depressed condition.

On another occasion our boat, striking across from Weti, where our tent was pitched, ran past the Island of Palms, and up a narrow circuitous swamp of mangroves, along a channel but a few feet wide, with trees standing in the salt water on both sides. The trees were loaded with long pods, and birds and fish had a happy time of it,

THE CASTLE, CHAKI-CHAKI, PEMBA.

T. Burtt, Photo.

unmolested. Steering our boat among this labyrinth of trees, we at last ran aground on the shore, and were carried on to the bank by our men at Matambwé. On reaching the sheikh's residence, four *askaris* with their guns were standing in the entrance-hall. We presented our papers, which were carefully read, the secretary or scribe afterwards returning us a written answer in Arabic to present to the authorities in Zanzibar.

Passing the attractive clumps of frangipani in full blossom in the shrubbery by the *baraza*, we found ourselves among the prolific fruit trees. Sheikh Naser-bin-Adi, of Matambwé, escorted us through his luxuriant shambas, amid fruitful groves of pomelo, orange, lime, citron, banana, pomegranates, cinnamon, cloves, and chillies. Up the tall palm trees the willing slaves climbed for *dafu*. The young cocoanut, which is full of delicious transparent *aqua coca*, provides a healthy beverage for travellers everywhere in these islands, and our four black boatmen returned in high spirits to their oars, laden probably with more spoils than any four of the twelve spies of Israel ever ventured to carry back with them from the land of promise.

The next day the sheikh paid us a return visit at our tent at Weti. Benjamin Edgington's tent was much admired; its interior fittings, beds, and mosquito-nets were examined; our table and chairs were in front, under the awning that formed the verandah. The position of our camp on the hill above Weti harbour, looking straight out to sea, was admirable. The tall cocoanut palms, with their feathery leaves fanning the breeze, afforded welcome shade; while the handsome clove trees and mangoes sheltered us from the north-east wind; and below us, on the slopes facing the sea, were the talipot palms, with their crowns of gigantic leafy fans. The sheikh had brought six armed *askaris* as an escort, and presented us with a sheep. The Arabs formed themselves into a crescent as they were grouped before us on chairs under the trees, in their picturesque turbans and their brilliantly coloured girdles, in which were belted their short, broad daggers with jewelled handle and scabbard. These Arab gentlemen are adepts in courtesy. As we rowed home in the evening, with the long shadows on the water, the sheikh and his men waited for us, started when we started, and accompanied our boat, taking the outer track as our guard, both sets of men pulling together to the same time, they to return to Matambwé as we struck southwards home. The Arab is a picturesque feature of East African life, and the English will not hastily or ruthlessly bid him disappear.

CHAPTER VI.

THE HINDU AS A SOCIAL FACTOR.

"Rest comes not except after hardship."—*Swahili Proverb.*

NOTHING strikes a stranger more with regard to the social life of Zanzibar and Pemba than the way in which the 5,600 East Indians have quietly taken possession of the trade and commerce of the islands. It appears to have arisen from the fact that the negroes, as being practically the slave class, were in no position to become the merchants and tradesmen of the community, and the aristocratic Arabs were already in position as landlords. The English who settled in the islands were for the most part Government officials or connected with Government offices, and there was little inclination on their part to select such an equatorial climate as a centre for promiscuous emigration. Therefore, while there is a sprinkling of German, French, Goanese, and Comorines, the trade of the country, by a sort of undesigned coincidence, has fallen into the hands of East Indians. Two or three circumstances tended in this direction; one being that Zanzibar and Pemba came under the protection of the same sovereign power as India; another that the rupee coinage of India was introduced by our Government as the coinage of Zanzibar; thirdly, that the people of India were inured to the hot climate of the tropics, and therefore settled more readily in an Oriental and tropical country such as Zanzibar. Hindus are not naturally inclined to emigrate or to cross the ocean, but the vast population of India is increasing so rapidly under our government that it must press out hither and thither if it is to thrive, and the more vigorous elements in Indian life move out on the crest of the wave of progress. Easy communication between Bombay and Zanzibar, and the constant transit to and fro of shipping, accelerated a movement which has developed to much larger proportions than any of our politicians contemplated. We therefore find ourselves in Zanzibar and Pemba in almost constant contact with Parsis, Khojas, Bohras, and Banyans.

One of the many delightful friendships we formed in the islands was with Bomanji Manekjee, the Minister of Public Works. Making his acquaintance in Zanzibar, and travelling with him afterwards on the *Barawa* to Pemba, we found him keenly interested in every public building that is being erected, whether a lighthouse, a landing-place, a custom-house, or a bungalow. He is also an enthusiastic naturalist, and devoted to the flora of the islands, especially to the introduction of new products, such as indiarubber, vanilla, and coffee. He seized a Ceylon book of ours on the cultivation of spices the moment he saw it, and, though a man of considerable conversational versatility, he vanished. He was found long afterwards in a chair on the verandah, intently reading the new-found source of information. His energy and executive ability have won the admiration of English officials; and officers who may find themselves listless and fever-stricken just in the crisis when a clear head and power for prompt action are requisite, gladly avail themselves of his services. Happy is the Government that has such a " man of activity " in its ministry.

THE PARSI CLUB, ZANZIBAR:
ASSEMBLY OF PARSI MERCHANTS AND THEIR WIVES IN THEIR PRIVATE PARK.

The Parsis have come to Zanzibar to stay. Many of them are wealthy. Their wives and families are well educated, and the Parsi Club, standing in its exquisitely beautiful grounds, adorned with palms, brilliantly coloured crotons, and giant tropical creepers, is one of the choicest spots in the suburbs. These Parsis, Khojas, Banyans, and Bohras, are all British subjects; and as such it has been illegal for them to hold slaves. This formerly placed the Indians at a disadvantage in holding land, and sometimes when a mortgage was foreclosed and the property fell into the hands of an East Indian, he was glad enough to let it to an Arab in order to get it cultivated. The consequence has been that the drift both of circumstance and of law has been to hem in the Indians to commerce and to money-lending. As money-lenders they have obtained an ill name in Zanzibar and Pemba for extortion and exorbitant demands; but everything points to a brighter day coming for the Hindu.

Money-lenders are unpopular the world over, whether in Europe, America, or India, whether Jews or Gentiles. There is not the slightest doubt that the Hindu money-lenders are extortionate, and as such are held up to common execration. Still the Arabs flee to them for loans, like flies to the flame. Listen to the description of Henry M. Stanley:—"The Banyan is a born trader, the beau-ideal of a sharp money-making man. Money flows to his pockets as naturally as water down a steep. No pang of conscience will prevent him from cheating his fellow-man. He excels a Jew, and his only rival in a market is a Parsi; an Arab is a babe to him. It is worth money to see him labour with all his energy, soul and body, to get advantage by the smallest fraction of a coin over a native. The Banyans exercise, of all other classes, most influence on the trade of Central Africa. With the exception of a few rich Arabs, almost all other traders are subject to the pains and penalties which usury imposes."* Mackay of Uganda gave similar testimony in writing to *The Times* in 1889: "Already in Zanzibar all the trade has passed into the hands of the Indians, which demonstrates the inability of the Arab to compete on fair terms with other traders."† J. S. Keltie, in speaking of the increase of trade in Zanzibar, says that in 1878 "British Indian traders, both Hindu and Mohammedan, of whom thousands were settled on the islands and on the coasts, were a powerful factor in the Sultanate."‡ During the succeeding twenty years the same feature has become intensified. The Arab has become weaker, continually increasing his indebtedness to the Indian mortgagee, while the Banyan, the Khoja, and the Hindu have acquired a firmer grip than ever on the trade of the islands.

Consul V. K. Kestell-Cornish gave us an introduction to two or three of the Khojas in Chaki-Chaki. It was curious to watch the look of pleased surprise with which they recognised the kindly courtesy thus bestowed upon them by Government. But when they read the document, and recognised that we were their fellow-subjects of the same good Queen Victoria, and that as such we met them in friendship and goodwill, they held out their hands to us and gave us a welcome that betokened the most hearty appreciation. It has been, perhaps, hardly sufficiently considered how very much the English Government owes to the trading classes of the country, who, though not its aristocracy, are, by their industry and economy, adding greatly to

* "How I Found Livingstone," page 12.
† "Mackay of Uganda," page 440.   ‡ "Partition of Africa," page 231.

its material wealth. No Government can afford to look askance at its workers; and of all the free people in East Africa none work harder or for longer hours than these East Indian tradesmen. England, after all, is herself the greatest money-lender the world has ever known. She lends to every nation, whether to her American cousins, to Asiatic and African mining and railway enterprises, or to necessitous European Powers. Perhaps it is to this very position as the world's greatest money-lender that England owes her unpopularity. But surely, if we see ourselves as others see us, we can afford to extend to our Indian fellow-subjects the generosity to appreciate the valuable services they are rendering to our trade in Zanzibar and in East Africa. Their industry is a tropical marvel. Their little shops are open very early in the morning, long before most of us are awake. Their store of baskets filled with oddments, and their exhibit of fancy soaps and mirrors, knives and glasses, cotton fabrics and ribbon, fruit and vegetables, are displayed and line the narrow streets. They do not leave their shop to others, but sit hour after hour cross-legged in the open front, sheltered from the sun. They make themselves a convenience to the public for whom they cater, and patiently abide their time till far into the evening. Such frugal people, diligent in business and attentive to detail, are sure to thrive; and as they thrive, the country in which they live is benefited.

Our morning hours were familiar with the constant chatter of one of these thriving Khojas, who transacted his business exactly on the opposite side of the street. He waylaid the country folks as they came into town laden with their sacks of copra. Tired with their load, they were glad to rest. Then came the long haggling about the price, the Khoja

A STREET SCENE IN CHAKI-CHAKI, PEMBA.

H. Armitage, Photo.

beating them down to a pice, and wasting more words on a pice than Englishmen would spend on a sovereign. Many an outburst of laughter would arise from the onlookers as one joke after another passed, the Khoja never yielding, but making up for it by abundant chatter. At last the price is fixed, and the load laid on the weighing machine. Vain are the protests that come from the countryman that the weight is incorrect. Thump go the weights upon the scales. The money jingles merrily in the Khoja's bag of coins. It is irresistible. The transaction is complete. The ready money changes hands, and another customer appears as a stalwart black servant, a sort of half-caste, carries to the rear of the shop the copra purchased, to make room for the next parcel.

Some of these country customers are Wa-Pemba. They form another of the curiosities of island life, being the aboriginal inhabitants. There is in the very existence of these people, in the presence of centuries of Arab occupation, something which almost puts to shame the Anglo-Saxon. In the Eastern States of America we may live for months without seeing a Red Indian. He has, alas! been civilised off the scene, though the white man has only been there a few generations. The Maories of New Zealand vanish before the English settler. The Arab, with all his slave-raiding and slave-dealing, has allowed the Wa-Pemba to maintain their settlements to the present day. In the midst of large Arab plantations, the aborigines still squat on their original holding, and carry on their cultivation as small independent landowners.

And now the English are the paramount power, or, as Lord Rosebery used to say, the predominant partner, and under our Protectorate all these races are to have fair play.

CHAPTER VII.

THE ENGLISH AS A SOCIAL FACTOR.

" The custom of a slave is to talk ; with the freeborn is action."
Swahili Proverb.

OUR rapidly growing home population must open out fresh channels for trade. Foreign competition, added to the increasing output resulting from perfected machinery, makes new markets essential. The acquisition, therefore, in Africa, of 2,194,880 square miles of territory, with a population of 43,227,700 (exclusive of Egypt), creates for England one of those outlets for trade which is an immense advantage to all commercial and manufacturing interests. While benevolently considering how much good we can do to the peoples we govern, in developing the magnificent natural resources these vast territories contain, we do not leave out of consideration the interests of our island home, the crowded central hive where every one must be fed. Forty-three million customers are not to be despised. This African population, after all, only gives an average of twenty persons to the square mile, while in India we find large territories that show 335, 387, 454, and 468 persons to the square mile. Africa is therefore not only dark, but it is undeveloped. The population on certain African areas, such as Zanzibar and Pemba, without overcrowding, shows 219 persons to the square mile, and there thus appears room for an indefinite increase of population in the vast fertile areas which are included in our African Protectorates.

As civilisation progresses, more and more of our cotton goods and other manufactures will be required.

Germany is devoting itself energetically to the development of its own acquisitions in East Africa; and while we may regret the iron heel of militarism which too often manifests itself in its dealings with native communities, it is a great pleasure to recognise that our German neighbours are forming a strong and most valuable Protectorate in East Africa. They have secured very important geographical positions, such as Kilimanjaro, and are developing their African dependency in a business-like manner. We had the privilege of making the acquaintance of a number of East African Germans, and found them courteous and energetic. The German Club in Zanzibar, which has now excellent accommodation, is a social force in the city. There is so much Teutonic blood in our own veins that it often seems as though the sober German colonist and pioneer was in many ways singularly akin to ourselves in tastes and disposition. He has just that stolid mental constitution and vigour that settles down to prosper and prevail.

It is, therefore, well that every citizen at home should recognise distinctly that the efficient administration of Zanzibar and Pemba and our other Protectorates tends materially to promote our own home interests. Mr. J. Chamberlain, in appealing to the working men of Birmingham in 1892 respecting East Africa, said with great force :—" All questions which affect the extension of the Empire have a very pressing interest for working men. Those people who want you to have a little Empire must make up their minds that with a little Empire will go a little trade. This United Kingdom of ours is, after all, but a small place,—it is but a mere speck upon the surface of the globe,—and it would be absolutely impossible that from our own resources alone we could find employment for our crowded population of forty millions of souls. No; your hope of continuous employment depends upon our foreign commerce; and now that other nations are closing their ports to us, and everywhere we see that they are endeavouring to create a monopoly for their own benefit, the future of the working classes in this country depends upon our success in maintaining the Empire as it at present stands, and in taking every wise and legitimate opportunity of extending it."* Captain Lugard speaks to the same effect:—"It has yet to be proved that the most effective way of relieving poverty permanently, and in accordance with sound political economy, is by distributing halfpence in the street. If our advent in Africa introduces civilisation, peace, and good government, abolishes the slave trade and effects other advantages for Africa, it must not be therefore supposed that this was our sole and only aim in going there. Though these may be our *duties*, it is quite possible that here, as frequently if not generally is the case, advantage may run parallel with duty."†

At present the English are experimenting with regard to the abundant commercial products of Zanzibar and Pemba. Copra and cloves are the two leading articles of export. The beautiful oil palm grows abundantly in many districts in Pemba, but is entirely neglected for purposes of trade. The cotton tree, which yields the *kapok* of commerce, grows luxuriantly to a height of sixty feet at Chaki-Chaki, but appears to be unused except for local purposes. The papaw, the jack-fruit, the areca-nut palm, sugar-cane, rice, and pineapples abound.

* *The Times*, June 2nd, 1892.
† "Rise of East African Empire," vol. i., page 381.

ZANZIBAR.

Whilst we do well to promote exports from Zanzibar of cloves, cinnamon, nutmegs, pimento, chillies, and indiarubber, we need to adhere firmly to the stipulations of the Brussels Act of 1891, guarding against the import of gunpowder and firearms, brandy and rum. Africa has been desolated by continual internecine war. Constant inter-tribal disputes have been fomented by the Arabs for the purposes of the slave trade. Africa knows little of peace until some firm Government steps in and interdicts the continual raiding of tribe upon tribe for purposes of plunder. As Captain Lugard says, " The *Pax Britannica* which shall stop this lawless raiding and this constant inter-tribal war will be the greatest blessing that Africa has known through the ages since the Flood."* On our arrival at Aden we transhipped from the Peninsular and Oriental steamer *Caledonia* into the steamer of another company for Zanzibar. Brandy and spirits were taken on board at Aden for East Africa, and as we sailed out of the bay we met by appointment a lighter carrying the red flag of danger, which was being towed by a steam launch. On this lighter were sixty-one cases of gunpowder and ammunition, which were all hoisted on board our steamer. Our personal safety as passengers, with such explosives below, might be a small matter; but to carry to East Africa such implements of destruction is a doubtful way of promoting commerce. Wilson's maxim in Africa was, " Always leave a country the better, if possible, for your having been in it."† Happily, our East Africa Protectorate has not been demoralised by the importation of intoxicating liquors to such an extent as some other parts of Africa. There is sufficient tendency among the people to indulge in strong drink without heavy importations from England.

* "Rise of East African Empire," vol. i., page 284.   † *Ibid*, page 336.

The *tembo* manufactured by the natives from the sap of the palm proved a sore temptation to our servants at Chaki-Chaki, although its sale is illicit.

Zanzibar does not present elements favourable for European colonists, although it derives great good from English influence. The climate is an effectual barrier to it ever becoming a popular resort for emigrants. Not that the temperature runs up to the high readings to which we are accustomed in India; but while these sea-girt isles have an unusually low range of temperature considering that they are within five degrees of the equator, the humidity of the air makes them liable to malarial fever. The north-east monsoon in January, February, and March is often very pleasant. It brings a refreshing, health-giving breeze that is a luxury in these three months, which are the hottest in the whole year, and the force of the wind is not usually violent. But the south-west monsoon, in April, May, and June, is very tempestuous. A hot, dreamy, languid atmosphere is not attractive to Englishmen. The whole of the east coast is bathed in warm ocean currents that materially affect the prevailing languor, and we shall probably learn with increasing acquaintance that we are quite as much influenced by these ocean currents as we are by atmospheric changes. One necessity is to avoid all unnecessary exposure to the sun. Five minutes wanton exposure of the head may result in illness. Cholera-belts of some sort are essential. Flannel is a protection against chills. Marshy lands are malarious after the rains. It is necessary that Europeans return home on furlough after three or four years' residence in the enervating climate of Equatorial Africa, to recover blood and nerve, muscle and tone.* But the work constantly done by our English merchants in Zan-

---

* R. M. Heanley's "Memoir of Bishop Steere."

zibar in the transaction of their business, and the activity in athletic sports, such as cricket, tennis, and golf, in which the Europeans of Zanzibar engage in the evenings, show that the possibility of health in the islands is more hopeful than at first sight appears.

The acquisition of Swahili, which is the one language of constant intercourse, is not an insuperable obstacle. It has its peculiarities, especially in the formation of its tenses. But words of common parlance are quickly learned; and the diligent use of the little is the highway for the acquisition of more. The new arrival as he enters a house cries "Hodi, Hodi," he salutes with the customary "Yambo," and ere long settles down contentedly exclaiming "M'zuri."

The presence of Englishmen is in itself an influence for liberation and deliverance. If there is any authority we replace, it is commonly the Arab slave-holder, or some petty native king. Let us ever remember that our incapacity may prove oppressive. The loathsome and seething impurity that festers under the ægis of Mohammedanism is rebuked in the presence of an Englishman. One pure English home, whether that of a Government official or of a missionary, introduces a higher standard and ideal of life. Such homes are in themselves a gospel. The influence of slavery on the Arabs has been terribly demoralising. Not only have the slaves been corrupted, but the physical stamina of their masters has been fatally vitiated. The Arab community is in process of decay. Men inquire cynically why so many mission converts break down and evince such instability of character. The answer is that it takes generations to purge out the old leaven. It is one of the strange mysteries of life that the iniquity of the fathers is visited to the third and the fourth generation upon their tempted and wrestling children.

The Englishman is not only needed in directing enterprise. He is quite as much required in the courts of justice. We have already seen, in considering the Arab, that the Wali and the Cadi are unreliable. The presence of an Englishman produces a revolution. We enter a local court. A man and his wife from Beloochistan have been living on a plantation, and one of the aboriginal Wa-Pemba claims part of the plantation as belonging to his ancestors. It is a civil case, brought forward for reconsideration. The dispute takes the form of two claimants for payment for the frasilas* of cloves that have been thrown on the market as the produce of the plantation. The lady who considers herself the heiress has her face partially concealed with the *barakoa* with its ornamented bars. A seat has been provided for her, while her husband, who is of milder temperament, sits cross-legged on the floor. The harem lady, who is eager for her little holding, has no restrictions of etiquette about pleading her own case, and is abundantly voluble and gesticular, with arms and jewelled hands adding emphasis to her feminine logic. To the left stands a witness, one of those strange half-breeds that find it their policy to side with the Arabs, although they have more negro blood in their veins than anything else. He happens to be a notorious slave-dealer, who has handled slaves as cattle, and bartered them almost all his life. He is a well-known old slave auctioneer. His face is a study of cool ferocity, a countenance that betrays nothing of what is working in his mind ; but one instinctively revolts from the imperious man. The tales of cruelty the man could tell if he chose to speak would defile the annals of any police-

* Four frasilas of 35lbs. = 140lbs. of cloves or one bale.

STREET SCENE, ZANZIBAR.

court. But he knows the country, he is more intimate with local circumstance than any Englishman can ever hope to be, and here he stands to give evidence. At the upper end sits cross-legged a thin old Arab judge. He has a gift for silence, but listens much, as he leans an elbow on one knee, supporting his chin with his hand. He has never been clothed with ermine, or worn a wig. He knows nothing of the precedents of Westminster, but appears thoughtfully endeavouring to unravel the case. At his side sits an astute Arab with a dagger in his girdle. He is the Wali, the most notable man in all Chaki-Chaki. His dagger was in past days the terror of the natives. With it the Arab was prepared on occasion to settle with all gainsayers. Now it is useless except to decorate its scabbard. In the Wali's hand are little strips of tough paper, from which he is reading supposed contracts and legal agreements. In this native court sits one English official. He has the pleas spread out on the table before him, and is attentively taking notes of the evidence on both sides. The little native farmer of the Wa-Pemba looks anxiously to this Englishman as to a superior being from whom alone he can ever hope for justice. Sentence after sentence of the evidence this little farmer gives is taken down by the white man, and the nervous countryman begins to gain a gleam of hope. As this countryman sits cross-legged on the floor giving evidence, his head and body rise up every now and then with emotion, something like the head of a snake in the midst of its coil. The Englishman cross-questions in Swahili, and investigates the case, but does not pronounce the official decision. The Wali and the Judge, however, courteously accept his advice. This is to the effect that two arbitrators shall be appointed to investigate the boundaries on the spot and inquire into ancient rights, that these two arbitrators shall have power to call in a third in case of need, and that their decision shall be final. Plaintiff and defendant pass out, satisfied that the decision is the best at which mortals can arrive upon the earth. Immediately afterwards two slaves enter in chains. Their master requests that they may be punished. He is unable to control them; he has repeatedly tried and failed. The Arab masters are quite accustomed to bring their negroes to the Wali to be punished. Evidence is given, and it appears clear that these men dig through the mud walls into the neighbours' houses at night, just as men used to do two or three thousand years ago : "In the dark they dig through houses which they had marked for themselves" (Job xxiv. 16). Their own account of their transactions is listened to, but it is evident they are guilty. They are sent to the whitewashed House of Correction. They look the picture of despair, but the verdict is right. They are very Ishmaelites. They consider every man's hand is against them, and their hand is against every man. Who shall teach them better so long as the iron heel of slavery prevails?

Thus where the Englishman goes in East Africa, whether among Arabs, Indians, half-breeds, or negroes, he aims at justice. The people of Pemba proverbially say, "An Englishman is a man who has righteousness," that is, he has an inherent sense of justice. Centuries of culture have made him an administrator. Under his rule diverse peoples thrive together. He binds races and tribes in concord and peace. He may have many faults, and is doubtless too little aware of them himself, but the resources of the country are developing, hope springs in the heart of depressed nationalities, and a brighter day is dawning upon those who have never yet known the benediction of peaceful civilisation.

As Lord Rosebery said at Glasgow on the 1st November, 1897 :—" Our Empire, as at present constituted, under the wise guidance of a free-trade policy, makes for peace, for commerce, and for enlightenment. But if you want the foundations of our Empire to be on sounder grounds still, if you wish to dig broader and deeper and stronger the foundations of this world-wide Empire, the home of all English peoples, you want something more even than peace and commerce and enlightenment. You must take care that the corner-stones of the majestic structure are not merely peace, but honour and *justice to subject races*, and fair dealing among the citizens, of whatever colour they may be, who live under your rule."

CHAPTER VIII.

GOVERNMENT BY PROTECTORATE.

"Those who do a work do not fail to have a reason."—Swahili Proverb.

ENGLAND, in becoming the dominant Power over vast territories in Africa, assumed heavy responsibilities, which, to some considerable extent, it is honestly endeavouring to fulfil. In India the chaotic condition of the various governments and the internal discord had led on to what England never intended. As Sir J. R. Seeley so well puts it, " We meant one thing and did quite another ; all along we have been looking one way and moving another." In Africa, instead of seizing early opportunities of conquest, successive English Administrations delayed for nearly sixty years the acquisition of territories that seemed waiting to fall into their hands, until at last there was among the European Powers a scramble for Africa without precedent. No other way appeared possible for stopping the constant internecine strife among African tribes, fomented by slave-traders. A far more cruel system than that of protectorate towards inferior races in the presence of rising civilised communities is that of extermination. Although some of our dealings with South African tribes have been ruthless and overbearing, we certainly have not committed the sin of extermination.

The complexity of our Eastern Protectorates lies in the presence of the Mohammedan Power. The Arabs are but a small portion of the population,

SLAVE GIRL BUYING FRUIT FROM A HINDU TRADESMAN.

yet it is through their machinery that we exercise control in Zanzibar and Pemba. This results in compromise with regard to social customs. Our government is patriarchal; Mohammedanism is despotic. The strange anomaly is therefore presented, of a strong democratic Power, accustomed to legislate through representative institutions, placing itself in intimate relationship with an antique despotism that was formerly a tyranny. But in our effort to obtain justice for the negro we have no right to be unjust to the Arab. Hence a government by protectorate often shapes its course as government by compromise. It is not easy, logically, to defend our position. Englishmen admire thoroughness. Courage of conviction, honesty of purpose, integrity in jurisprudence, we reverence. We have to hark back to the position we started with in our first chapter—that our legislation in East Africa is in a state of transition; that existing arrangements may be serviceable for a time, and that revolutionary changes are not always beneficial. Protectorates are not an unmixed evil, but they are not ideal. They are ameliorating the open sore of a vast continent. The Sultan signs a decree, the Englishman guides the hand. A Mohammedan judge pronounces a verdict, the Englishman predicates the decision.

England, as a paramount Power, served an apprenticeship to a slightly analogous system in allowing the native States to remain under native princes in India. Our blunders with our kith and kin in America, and the consequent establishment of the great Anglo-Saxon Republic, were trials that taught us moderation and consideration. It sounds presumptuous for European Powers to sit down at a table and evolve the partition of Africa without consulting the peoples concerned. Yet the result is proving beneficial. Extraordinary and unprecedented as the process may seem, it is leading to Africa's redemption. Thus the aspirations and prayers of Livingstone, Mackay, and Hannington find fulfilment. To plant in the midst of these mixed populations men of character who work for righteousness, men that despise the gain of oppression, and that shake their hands from holding of bribes, is in itself a great boon. The natives show their appreciation of the "love of fair play" which has characterised our officials in East Africa. Another boon conferred by our administration is security. At home we are so accustomed to enjoy security that we scarcely appreciate its value.

The influence of England has been exercised for many years in the mitigation of slavery and in withstanding the slave trade. In these efforts other European Powers have assisted. The first united effort of this description was the Berlin Conference of 1885. In this remarkable Conference, Germany, Austria, Belgium, Denmark, Spain, France, England, Italy, Portugal, the Netherlands, Russia, Norway and Sweden, Turkey, and the United States were all represented. This comprehensive gathering assembled " in the name of Almighty God," declaring their object to be to settle in a spirit of mutual goodwill the most favourable conditions for the development of commerce and civilisation in Africa, and to promote the moral and material welfare of the native races. By the Berlin Act of February 26th, 1885, the Conference guaranteed liberty of conscience and religious toleration, offered "special protection" to Christian missionaries, the free and public exercise of every creed, and the right to erect religious buildings and organise missions. It agreed to co-operate in the suppression of slavery. The slave trade was forbidden under Article 9, all the Powers undertaking to employ every means to put an end to the traffic. Valuable concessions were entered into with regard to free trade, insisting on moderate charges on the rivers and on the coast, such charges being merely of the character of remuneration for services rendered. The object of these stipulations was essentially philanthropic, and tended to the encouragement of future commercial enterprises in the interior. King Leopold II. devoted assiduous attention to the problems of the Congo State, and Prince Bismarck contributed to the good results of the Conference by his patient consideration in dealing with new proposals; while Baron de Courcel displayed great tact as President. The Berlin Act remains as a noble monument of one of the most unique gatherings of the Powers of Europe that ever assembled in the interests of mankind. Hereafter the regenerated peoples of Africa may look back to the Berlin Act of 1885 as the Magna Charta of their enfranchisement.

Meanwhile the Powers were learning more and more of the actual requirements for the government of this vast continent. It was in many ways an experiment in government on a scale utterly unprecedented in human history. It aimed at the moral and social regeneration of millions of untutored beings, who were themselves essential to the development of their own country, but who could not be personally consulted. Instead of the brutalities of pure aggression, it was recognised that tropical Africa, if it was ever to become "the garden of the Lord," must be developed by the sinews of Africans themselves. The Powers of Europe, while recognising the advantages that must come to the peoples of Europe by the development of commerce, also acted in the spirit of goodwill and

ON THE SHAMBA.

philanthropy towards the swarthy tribes who must do the work.

It is, therefore, not surprising that another Conference was proposed by Lord Salisbury in 1888, which assembled at Brussels in 1889, and continued its sittings till the 2nd July, 1890. In this Conference further important steps were taken in the same direction as those which had been entered upon in Berlin. The despatch of Lord Salisbury to Lord Vivian, our Ambassador at Brussels, on the 17th September, 1888, reflects credit on his genuine regard for anti-slavery interests. He suggested that the King of the Belgians invite a Conference to concert measures for "the gradual suppression of the slave trade on the continent of Africa, and the immediate closing of all the external markets which it still supplies." Two proposals were involved in this despatch, the one to be carried out "gradually," the other to take "immediate" effect, the suppression of the slave trade in such a vast continent by foreign Powers being necessarily the work of years, while the closing of the external slave-markets was, for the most part, within the range of immediate practical politics. Lord Salisbury emphasised the difficulties that had been encountered in the efforts of the cruisers of England to clear the seas of the traffic; and while stating that our Government would cheerfully continue "to bear the burden of further measures to effect the common object," it was evident that the system of "policing" the high seas had proved of but little efficacy towards actually suppressing the slave trade. A point was gained when it was thus conceded that our navy could do comparatively little in closing the traffic while slave-markets were open and the active demand for slaves continued.

The preamble of the Brussels Act of 1890 prominently declares the firm intention of the signatory Powers to " end the crimes and devastations engendered by the traffic in African slaves, protecting effectively the aboriginal populations of Africa, and ensuring for that vast continent the benefits of peace and civilisation." For these purposes it declared the most effective means to be the supplanting of human porterage by better and cheaper means of transport, such as railways, steamboats, and the construction of good roads. It advocated the establishment of telegraphic lines, and administrative posts and stations from point to point. It proceeded to impose restrictions on the importation of firearms, at least of modern pattern, and of ammunition, throughout the territories infected by the slave trade. Lastly, though not least, the Conference restricted the importation of and traffic in spirituous liquors. The Brussels Act, as Captain Lugard has observed, " vastly increases our obligations and defines them in greater detail." The enthusiasm of King Leopold in the development of the Congo State doubtless stirred up others to effort.

The edicts and agreements entered into in the direction of suppressing the slave trade and hemming in slavery in our East Africa Protectorate claim consideration. They fell far short of the desires of the people of England, who aimed at nothing short of full emancipation; but they represent an honest endeavour to restrain the evil. It was the new breath of Christianity playing through the old reed-pipes of Islam. These documents practically formulate themselves under three heads: *(a)* Edicts which were efforts to abolish the slave-trade; *(b)* Edicts and agreements to ameliorate the condition of the slave; and *(c)* Edicts tending in the direction of ultimate emancipation. One of the first important Zanzibar treaties on the slave trade was that entered into on the 5th June, 1873, between our Government and Seyyid Burghash, in which the Sultan agreed that the sea-borne traffic of slaves from the mainland " shall entirely cease." He further engaged that all slave-markets in his dominions should be closed. It is needless to add that this treaty did not stop the traffic. On the 14th July, 1875, a further treaty was made that all vessels carrying slaves other than those in attendance on their masters or employed in the navigation of the ship might be seized by Her Majesty's cruisers and condemned. In 1876 the Sultan issued another proclamation forbidding slave caravans from the interior.

In 1888, Colonel C. B. Euan-Smith, the Consul-General at Zanzibar, issued a proclamation declaring it illegal for any British subject to contract with the owner for the hire of any slave. The following year the Sultan Khalifa proclaimed the perpetual right of English and German vessels to search all Arab dhows for slaves, decreeing that all slaves brought into the dominions of Zanzibar after the 1st November, 1889, should be free. A further agreement was entered into between Sir Gerald Portal and the Sultan Khalifa, providing that all children born in the Sultan's dominions after the 1st January, 1890, should be free. This agreement, however, does not appear to have been embodied in any public proclamation.

Yet another decree was issued by the Sultan Ali-bin-Said on the 1st August, 1890, which contained important stipulations " in the name of God the merciful and the compassionate," providing that all slaves lawfully possessed at that date shall remain with their owners, and " their status shall be unchanged," but that all sale, purchase, or

SCENE ON PLANTATION.

exchange of slaves was henceforth absolutely prohibited. Any slave-broker was to be severely punished and exiled. Slaves might henceforth only be inherited by the lawful children of the deceased. If the deceased had no children, all his slaves became free. Cruelty inflicted on slaves by an Arab was to result in the forfeiture of all his slaves. No slave that was freed could ever after legally hold slaves. Slaves might purchase their freedom at a reasonable price, and papers of freedom were to be granted to them. Most of these stipulations were in the right direction, but the clause in the decree which affirmed that the status of the slaves " shall be unchanged " was afterwards used by Lord Salisbury in his despatch as an argument in favour of granting "compensation" to the Arabs, when the abolition of the legal status took place in 1897. This argument was on the ground that the decree had been issued under the advice of Sir C. Euan Smith. On such an assumption our British Consuls would be involved in almost immeasurable responsibilities. If the advice of an English Consul to a Mohammedan ruler ties the hands of future Administrations, and the nation is made responsible for his advice, it becomes the whole nation to watch most vigilantly every action of our Consular authorities abroad. Such an episode illustrates the serious complications involved in a civilised Government attempting to carry out its functions through a local Mohammedan administration. The penalty of a Sultan's clause which was in direct antagonism to the established antislavery policy of our country for more than half a century is thus inflicted upon us to-day.

In the face of all these edicts, slavery continued in operation in Zanzibar. The Sultans themselves were large slave-owners, and almost all the Arab authorities were interested in maintaining the system. But the edicts, and the action resulting from them, had the result of materially narrowing down the extent of the slave trade; and as the slave trade declined, the number of slaves on the islands steadily decreased, and slavery itself was being hemmed in.

The benevolent arrangement which Sir Gerald Portal made, that all children born in the Sultan's dominions after 1st January, 1890, should be free, had an unforeseen effect. It became the interest of slave-owners that their negroes should have no children. One of the most fearful effects of slavery is its disregard of the sanctities of home life. The slave has no home that he can call his own. His master may intrude upon it at any moment. The effect of slavery in Africa, as a rule, has been to discourage the birth of children; but for the masters to allow their slaves to rear children on whom the masters had no legal claim, presented a still greater temptation to underhand conduct. In very many cases the agreement was utterly ignored. In some instances the slaves were mutilated by their masters to prevent them having any children. There was also a terrible amount of infanticide. A mistress finding that a child absorbed the attention of a slave-mother, has been known to throw the child into a boiling caldron and destroy it. Hence the total result by the year 1895 was that many slaves had died, others had escaped, few raw slaves had been smuggled in, the rearing of children had been discountenanced, and the total number of slaves had very materially decreased. The Arab masters consequently hardly knew how to gather in their crops.

In the year 1890 a distinct epoch in the history of our relations to East Africa had been reached.

GOVERNMENT BY PROTECTORATE.

In the summer of that year, after conferring with European Powers, the British Protectorate was proclaimed over Zanzibar and Pemba. In October, 1891, an administration was instituted, worked by British officials, and under the supervision of Her Majesty's Agent and Consul-General. On the 1st February, 1892, Zanzibar was declared a free port. On the 2nd April, 1892, the Brussels Act came into operation, and the Directors of the British East Africa Company on the mainland took early steps to put its stipulations in force against the importation of arms and gunpowder and alcoholic liquors. On the 22nd June, 1892, our Government sent a notification to the signatories of the Berlin Act, informing them that from the 1st July the dominions of the Sultan of Zanzibar would be placed within the Free Zone with regard to imports. Consequent upon these arrangements, the appointment of the next Sultan, on the death of Ali-bin-Saïd, was by the authority of the English Government, which had become the protecting Power. Under our Protectorate, the Sultan of Zanzibar receives a fixed sum and retains his private estates, and the public revenues are wholly administered by British officers, under the direction of Sir Arthur Hardinge, the Consul-General.

DRYING CLOVES AT BANANI.

H. Armitage, Photo.

CHAPTER IX.

THE WIDER OUTLOOK.

"The beginning presents delays, then comes a downpour."
Swahili Proverb.

Whilst the scope of our inquiry is with regard to the welfare of Zanzibar and Pemba and of our East Africa Protectorate, it seems essential that we should recognise the problem as part of the larger and greater movement throughout the Dark Continent. It is, therefore, expedient to take a wider outlook. There are a multitude of tribes of very different mental and physical calibre, yet the difficulties we are called to face in one district find their counterpart, to a large extent, in many other districts; and though the climate of so vast an area differs greatly, the civilisation of the native tribes of Africa everywhere present many similar problems. It is this comparative condition of things that makes the work and experience of the specialist in one locality helpful to workers in other localities.

There may have been something that savours of romance, and much that savours of national ambition, in the rapid taking up by the European Powers of claims in Africa; but we confess that we believe there is also in it much that marks the hand of God. Great national impulses may contain in them something of the Divine, although their human outcome is often discouraging. Perhaps it would be too much to assume that from the bleeding heart of Africa went up a great cry unto God. We are certainly treading on surer ground when we assert that missionary after missionary who fell as martyrs to a treacherous climate, cried to God, and to comrades at home, on behalf of the Dark Continent. One of the most sublime illustrations of consecration to a great cause—to the greatest cause—has been the fact that volunteers for missionary service in Africa doubled and quadrupled, as one after another of those who had previously gone out laid themselves down to die. No clash of arms has ever revealed nobler courage and fuller persistence of purpose than modern missions in Africa. Yet there may be something nobler in carefully studying the laws of health in the tropics, and going to Africa to *live* rather than in hazarding life by ignorance, and going to Africa to die. Many lives might doubtless have been saved if men had observed the limitations of African environment; but it was almost inevitable in the low coast stations in the tropics, and in the great waterways of the interior, that lives should have been sacrificed. There are large areas of Africa that are not adapted to European immigration. Yet in such districts it seems essential to progress that some Europeans should reside as missionaries and Government officials, to introduce Christianity and civilisation. Portions of South Africa do, however, offer great natural inducements to Anglo-Saxon enterprise, and are well suited for colonisation.

The waterways of Africa presented the first means of access to the interior; and its great rivers, the Congo, the Nile, the Niger, and the Zambesi, must ever be important channels of intercourse. But we probably shall owe still more, in the onward march of African civilisation, to the gigantic inland lakes, which have become the romantic admiration of Europe. Lake Victoria, with its kindred Lakes

Albert Nyanza and Albert Edward, form nature's great reservoirs of the Nile, and the Lakes Nyasa and Tanganyika are manifestly destined to become the pathway of many a merchant steamer that shall bring light and hope and prosperity to the dark races of the interior; while marshy lakes such as Chad and Rudolf may become of more commercial utility than at present appears.

It certainly becomes every man who has an average interest in the welfare of his fellow-man to make himself to some extent acquainted with the recent history of African development. We need say little, and with the exception of Egypt men can say little accurately, with regard to the ancient history of Africa. Its interior was a *terra incognita*. Carthage and its northern shores played no mean part and exerted no small influence on the destinies of the Mediterranean. The early Christian Churches had many bishoprics, with a multitude of adherents, in North Africa. Except the Copts in Egypt, these have mostly vanished. Instead of religious efforts, Africa has been for generations exploited by the European Powers as the great hunting-ground for slaves. For generations no country was more guilty of this awful traffic than England. So early as 1562 Sir John Hawkins fitted out three ships to engage in the slave trade. The Portuguese and Spaniards had been before him, and Queen Elizabeth was justly indignant at Englishmen engaging in such an undertaking. But commercial greed prevailed. In the course of a century slaves came to be considered the principal commodity of merchandise from Africa, and there arose a constant rivalry among English, Dutch, and Spanish merchants to obtain a monopoly of the slave markets. In the face of this sorrowful record, it is a comfort to believe that the European

Powers have given evidence of genuine repentance, and by their later efforts to stem the stream of sorrow they have manifested a more conscientious regard for the rights of man.

While Great Britain now dominates 2,194,880 square miles, exclusive of Egypt, France claims 3,326,790 square miles; Portugal and Spain 980,000 square miles; Germany 884,810 square miles; and the Congo State, under the care of Belgium, covers 905,000 square miles. These are the leading Powers in African advance, although Italy has her claims in Somaliland and Abyssinia, and the Boers have their Republic in the South. The French are very active in West Africa, and are extending their territory as rapidly as circumstances permit. Their ambition appears to be to run a railway direct from Algiers across the Sahara to Senegal, and to the Gold Coast on the Gulf of Guinea. But the value of territory cannot in Africa be reckoned by area, and the fertile portions held by England are of infinitely greater value than much of the desert claimed by France.

Algeria is one of the most delightful parts of all Africa, and is a fascinating health-resort. It is very accessible from London, and a good service of steamers continually runs from Marseilles. It is the easiest spot for English people to visit who wish to see something of African life. The Moorish element in the city of Algiers is extremely picturesque. There are large and comfortable hotels at the capital, and 2,925 miles of railway open. Oranges, citrons, and palms abound. To some of us in past years a visit to Algeria has been like a beautiful revelation of the abundant goodness of God to man. But as a colony Algeria has not proved an abiding-place for any large number of Frenchmen. The French have not succeeded so well in the colonisation of their own acquired territories in Africa as they have in mingling with us in our Dominion of Canada. It cost France £150,000,000 to conquer Algeria, and it will be a long time ere she can recoup herself. Yet it is far better for France to devote her energies and skill to the development of her African Colonies than to involve herself in European jealousies.

The future of Africa is to a large extent in the hands of England and Germany. Whether Belgium will ultimately be able to control the Congo Free State remains to be seen; and apparently France can only make headway by a larger outlay from national resources than it can afford to invest. The two competitive Powers in the future of Africa are therefore Germany and England.

The Germans have three large areas of control—in the Cameroons, in its South-West territory, and in East Africa. They often make excellent colonists. The quiet plod of the homish German, as he settles down on his holding with his family of healthy boys and girls, shows how near of kin he is to the Englishman. He picks up languages more readily than his insular cousins, but has just the same faculty for trade, and is not so fastidious in his tastes. In East Africa the Germans are distinctly advancing. They are persistent competitors of English trade, and they are intelligent administrators.

The growing prosperity of Egypt under English control is a testimony to our kindly administration. The predominating control of the Nile Valley and of the Suez Canal is of great strategic value to England, and our recent successes and expenditure of resources in the Soudan make the evacuation of Egypt on our part an increasingly remote probability. The question whether this is an

CHAKI-CHAKI, PEMBA.

ultimate gain to the well-being of mankind may safely remain in abeyance; but the administration of Egypt under the dominant influence of England has greatly improved both its financial and agricultural resources. Egyptian finance now stands in a position of acknowledged security, the revenue exceeding the expenditure. Its agricultural products consist of cotton, maize, wheat, rice, sugar, hemp, &c. There are 958 miles of railway open to traffic. Irrigation works have been greatly developed, and the *corvée* or forced labour system has been abolished, except in cases of great emergency, such as guarding the banks of the Nile in floods. The present flourishing condition of Egypt has been unparalleled for thousands of years. Those who have stood in the tombs of the heroes of ancient Egypt, surrounded by their historic hieroglyphics, and have watched the elevation in recent years of the *fellahin* from serfdom to a measure of social privilege, cannot but rejoice in the change that has taken place under our administration.

In South Africa we have become embroiled in a series of unhappy conflicts with the aborigines that are humiliating to the Christian and discreditable to the aggression of colonials. We have little cause to point the finger at others, when we have so disgracefully beaten back the native tribes in South Africa, and allotted their fertile lands to our own emigrants, and when we are still permitting so much injustice to continue in the treatment of Zulus and Kaffirs. The administration of Cape Colony, with its healthy surroundings, has been followed by the successive acquisition of Natal and Zululand, of Bechuanaland, Basutoland, Matabeleland, and Mashonaland, and of British Central Africa, until we have in round numbers nearly one million square miles under our control in South Africa. In East Africa and Somaliland, with its adjuncts, we have 737,000 square miles. The Niger and Gold Coast territories in West Africa cover other 481,000 square miles, with a population in West Africa alone of about thirty millions. There are elements in our position on the Niger and the Gold Coast and Sierra Leone that naturally awaken the keen interest of Englishmen. In the seventeenth and eighteenth centuries it was to the West Coast that the attention of Europe and of America was mainly directed. There we encountered an amount of competition that stimulated the British mind to activity and resourcefulness. It is more than a century since British traders settled on the Oil Rivers, and, to our shame be it spoken, mainly for the purposes of the slave trade. Eager explorations of the Niger regions were running on from the year 1815. For half a century British missionaries have been at work in Calabar. But the attitude of England was wavering and halting, while other European Powers, especially France and Germany, were pushing forward their expeditions in West Africa. The consequence is that the map of West Africa to-day presents much the appearance of a dissecting puzzle. It is not easy to explain the curious delimitations of territory which now exist under various European "Agreements." In many instances they are the result of compromises. Taking all things into consideration, we may be thankful that the delimitation of boundaries in Africa has been effected by mutual conciliations, rather than by the old-time custom of going to war. The result is that while England has abundant estates in Africa, which may take her many generations to develop, she has frequently surrendered districts to other Powers that at one time seemed naturally, by the residence of her merchants, to be in her keeping.

J. Scott Keltie, to whose able work on "The Partition of Africa" every student of Africa is greatly indebted, says:—"In the building up of our world-wide Empire we have no doubt done many things which we ought not to have done, and left undone many things which we ought to have done. Yet the name of our country still stands high among our less-advanced brothers in Africa for many of those qualities which exalt a nation."* May the new era upon which we have entered in the Dark Continent not only reflect great credit upon our national honour, but may our highest achievement be that we have liberated the African from the slavery and degradation of centuries, that we have opened channels for commercial development and civilisation that shall make his emancipation a genuine redemption, and above all, that we have brought to at least part of Africa the glad tidings of Christianity!

* "Partition of Africa," page 517.

BANANI ESTATE, LOOKING ACROSS BAY.

H. Armitage, Photo.

CHAPTER X.

THE ABOLITION OF THE LEGAL STATUS OF SLAVERY.

"My Creator and Preserver tries His slave and then opens the way before him."—*Swahili Proverb.*

"THE logical sequence" of the various edicts and agreements which had been passed by the Sultans of Zanzibar was the abolition of the legal status of slavery in 1897.* The conscience of England on the slavery question was much more fully developed than in the days of our forefathers. Christians no longer argued the advantages of slavery as they argued even in our own childhood. The British and Foreign Anti-Slavery Society has not yet seen the fruition of its travail of soul, but it has seen a marked change for the better in public opinion and in the official mind. Slave-trading and slave-raiding have been greatly reduced in proportions, although in the interior of Africa they are still far from extinct. The abolition of the legal status of slavery had worked well in India. Clauses 2, 3, 4 of the Indian Act of 1843 are to this purport:—2. No rights arising out of an alleged property in the person and service of another as a slave shall be enforced by any civil or criminal court or magistrate. 3. No person who may have acquired property by his own industry, or by the exercise " of any art, calling, or profession, or by inheritance, assignment, gift, or bequest, shall

---

* Instructions to Mr. Hardinge (now Sir Arthur Hardinge, K.C.M.G.) respecting the abolition of the legal status of slavery in the islands of Zanzibar and Pemba, Africa, No. 1 (1897).

be dispossessed of such property, or be prevented from taking possession thereof, on the ground that such person, or that the person from whom the property may have been derived, was a slave."

4. "Any act which would be a penal offence if done to a free man, shall be equally an offence if done to any person on pretext of his being in a condition of slavery."

While the circumstances in Zanzibar and Pemba differed materially from the position in India, it was felt that the time had come to adopt in those islands regulations which should have a somewhat similar effect to the Indian Act of 1843. It was intended to avoid any violent dislocation of the labour market. The previous edicts of various Sultans had prepared the way for more comprehensive legislation; and though the edicts in several directions failed to achieve their purpose, owing to the immobility of Mohammedan and African custom, there had been working among the people other elements which had resulted in the betterment of the slaves. The influence of English authority in the islands had greatly increased. The presence of English officials as well as of missionaries had the effect of throwing light on dark corners, where cruelty and oppression could no longer hide. The quiet and firm effort of such men as Sir John Kirk, Sir Gerald Portal, and General Sir Lloyd William Mathews had done much to prepare the way for abolition; while the protests of Bishop Steere, and more recently of Bishop Tucker, were ploughing up the fallow ground and leavening the Arabs themselves with maturer thoughts. The commercial depression which resulted from the reduced price of cloves also greatly affected the Arabs. English control, combined with the edicts, had greatly reduced the number of slaves available for cultivating the shambas. The incubus of heavy mortgages on the estates impoverished the slave-holders, and the estates themselves yielded small profit. Thus the Arabs were more than ever prepared for change, and were themselves recognising that emancipation, accompanied with the introduction of free labour, lay straight before them.

Public opinion in England played an important part in the current that was setting in towards emancipation. Yet in some ways there had been for years in England a lethargy with regard to continued protest against slavery. An opinion appeared for some time to prevail that slavery had been extinguished from British territory, that in the United States the throes of civil war had resulted in emancipation, and that our national responsibilities respecting it to a large extent had ceased. A multitude of other pressing questions had claimed precedence in public attention, and a lull was evident, which was disturbed by the rapid partition of Africa among the European Powers, by which we assumed fresh responsibilities respecting native tribes that were being decimated by the slave trade.

But as accurate and intimate knowledge of our African Protectorates increased in England, the electorate awoke to the existing evils of slavery, and neither Liberal nor Conservative Administrations could long avoid the issue. The Liberal Cabinet stood committed to an anti-slavery policy; and Lord Salisbury, when previously in power, had done good service in the same direction. It was consequently with the clear recognition of "the force of public opinion in this country" that the despatch of 10th February, 1897, was sent by the Foreign Secretary to Zanzibar. Various forces, both at home and abroad, thus culminated in the Sultan's proclamation in favour of emancipation. On the forefront of Lord Salisbury's despatch he stated that it was issued in fulfilment of pledges which had been " given in Parliament for the abolition of the legal status of slavery in the islands of Zanzibar and Pemba." The conclusion of the despatch announced that the object of the Government was " that the legal status of slavery in the islands should cease henceforward to exist, that the change should be effected without injustice to individuals, and at the same time without detriment to the public welfare." The basis of the proposals impressed upon the Sultan of Zanzibar were given under nine brief headings, formulating the results of much careful consultation with Sir Arthur Hardinge and other officials. Their substance is as follows :—

1. A decree should be at once issued abolishing the legal status of slavery in the islands of Zanzibar and Pemba.

2. An assurance should be given in this decree that no interference is contemplated in family life.

3. Her Majesty's Government do not recommend any form of apprentice labour.

4. Compensation should be awarded by the Zanzibar Government to such owners of slaves as can prove legal tenure of any of their slaves under Clause 2 of the decree of 1890, and damage resulting from abolition.

5. Compensation money should not be seizable for past debt.

6. Her Majesty's Government will lend the services of British officers to watch the cases and to prevent injustice.

7. A renewed attempt will be made to procure coolie labour from India.

8. The Zanzibar Government should immediately adopt such measures of a police or precautionary character as may prevent social or financial disorder, and secure the successful operation of the decree.

9. Her Majesty's Government are hopeful that the change may be effected without risk, and at no considerable cost. In the event, however, of a serious strain being placed upon the resources of the Zanzibar Government, they would be prepared to consider the question of financial aid.

It is clear from the above that the intention of our Government was the undoubted abolition of the legal status of slavery. A definite step of great value was thus taken, from which it was practically impossible to recede. So far back as 1884, Sir John Kirk, then acting as Consul-General in Zanzibar, stated, in addressing the authorities at home, that "the non-recognition of slavery as a status known to the law is essential to prosperity in Pemba." One point at which abolitionists had been aiming for many years was thus attained. A great deal was left to accomplish, but the Rubicon had been passed so far as Zanzibar and Pemba were concerned. With additional satisfaction it was noted that Lord Salisbury had concluded not to recommend or recognise any form of apprentice labour in lieu of slavery.

On the 14th November, 1896, a large deputation of Friends had waited upon the Right Hon. G. N. Curzon, M.P., Under-Secretary for Foreign Affairs, to protest against any system of "apprenticeship" being adopted in Pemba and Zanzibar which should have the effect of still binding the slaves to their masters. In that deputation, which was ably introduced by Joseph Albert Pease, M.P., it was shown from past experience that Sir John Kirk was

MAKUTI HUTS ON FRIENDS' ESTATE, BANANI.

H. Armitage, Photo.

perfectly right in his axiom that " the two systems of slave and free labour will never blend." Slavery shuts out free labour from the market, because independent working men will not work where labour is degraded by compulsion. The Government courteously accepted the plea of the deputation, and an important step was gained.

On the matter of compensation there was more difficulty. The whole spirit of Christianity appears opposed to slavery, and in the onward march of Christianity slavery must disappear. Every man, unless by crime he forfeits freedom, has the natural right to liberty; and if compensation is granted with regard to abolition, it would appear that it is the slave that should receive the compensation. We cannot, therefore, regard compensation to the slave-owner as in itself logical. These slaves have many of them been torn from their homes by cruel raiders, and the man who buys them is a guilty accomplice.

It was perfectly right not unnecessarily to interfere with family life, but a slave women requires quite as much legal protection, or even more, than a man. Undoubtedly, Arab notions of morality present a serious difficulty. The dual character of the Government renders legislation very difficult when it has to do with long-established social customs. The decree is issued by the Sultan; the hand that guides the pen is in Downing Street. How long such a complicated and cumbrous system can last is uncertain. But to deny to women the power to claim freedom is cruel and immoral. On one page of the despatch Lord Salisbury says distinctly that " on and after the date at which it is to come into operation, no Court shall recognise any claim to the service of *any* person on the ground of the latter's alleged servile status." On the next page of the same despatch he says: "It has been pointed out that if the proposed abolition were to extend to the women of the harem and to the connubial system upon which the Arab family is founded, an opposition would be aroused that would enlist upon its side the stubbornest and most cherished convictions of the Arab nature." It would seem here as though two separate issues were mixed together. If a woman in the harem, or a concubine, being a slave, desires to be free from her master, she surely ought to have the protection of the Government in claiming her freedom. If a woman so circumstanced, on the other hand, desires to remain with her master, she ought not to be compelled to leave him. The Government has no right to compel her to stay or to compel her to go. But the Government ought to provide for the liberty and emancipation of women just as much as for men. In the compromise that is now attempted a temptation is opened for Arabs to claim as their concubines women who might otherwise be free. The decree might have been allowed to work itself out without the insertion of any compromising restriction whatever respecting concubines. Lieutenant C. S. Smith, late Vice-Consul at Zanzibar, states the whole matter clearly when he says: "Being subject to the irresponsible will of the master, a girl cannot be virtuous." "To a girl brought up in slavery, chastity is impossible even before her childhood ends. Chastity is impracticable for a woman enslaved by force, for the simple reason that her body is not her own."* When we consider that far more than one-half of the 140,000 slaves in Zanzibar and Pemba were women, it seems wrong that the Arab masters should have the

* "History of Universities' Mission," page 426.

option of claiming any of them as concubines who desire deliverance. We cannot believe the Christian conscience of England will tolerate such an exemption in the working of the Act. Not that we imagine that this exemption will result in all the women being claimed by the Arabs. Many of the Arabs will doubtless allow women to obtain their freedom and go. But the desecration of home life is one of the most awful iniquities of slavery, and it may take generations before a population that has been so long tainted with immorality will become pure.

Though every female slave *may* become a concubine, only a limited number are really made so. A concubine has certain defined rights. She has apartments of her own, is free at her master's death, and confers freedom and legitimacy on her offspring. Few respectable Arabs would allow their concubines to engage in menial work. To do so would be repugnant to their sense of propriety, and to the feeling of jealousy with which they regard their harems. The number of concubines is, therefore, largely dependent on an Arab's pecuniary resources; and in the present impoverished condition of the Arab community it is hardly to be expected that he will add to his encumbrances by any large accession of concubines. The Courts naturally would not recognise a woman as a concubine, especially where the question of compensation is involved, unless it could be shown that she had occupied a definite and perfectly ascertainable status as such before the case arose.

The great difficulty regarding native women is for the most part in their exceedingly dependent position. They are usually dependent on their masters for the means of subsistence, and it requires unusual force of character and boldness for them to strike out a new course of their own. At the same time, various occupations, such as water-carriers and washerwomen, are open to them, and many of them in the country are accustomed to field work. Nevertheless, they greatly lack the moral qualities which have been the making of the noble mothers of our Anglo-Saxon communities, and these qualities are not often attained in one or two generations. The more urgent is the need for Christian women to rise to the succour of their coloured sisters, and to go forth as missionaries and stand by them in their terrible struggle for a higher and purer standard of life. Native women who obtain their freedom through the influence of our English Government will need moral support after they have obtained deliverance from slavery. The perils of freedom to such women are great. Councils of cowardice appear to have been listened to with regard to the exemption of so many negro women from the privileges of the decree for the abolition of the legal status of slavery. To offer emancipation to men, while leaving women in compulsory concubinage, for fear of Arab opposition, betrays ungallant timidity. While we heartily commend Lord Salisbury for the forward steps he has taken, we regret he was influenced to interpose limitations which rob so many who need it most of the privileges of the decree.

Bishop Tucker's criticism in *The Times* for 12th April, 1897, has great force. He says: "Slavery in East Africa dies hard." He then states his three objections to the despatch : firstly, the continued enslavement of many of the women ; secondly, the limited freedom granted to the men by suggested restrictions respecting their leaving the islands ; and thirdly, that the action of the decree is confined to the islands of Zanzibar and Pemba, not including Mombasa and the territories on the mainland within the ten-miles strip. This latter point has been contested in the House of Commons by Joseph A. Pease; and the Government, through Mr. A. J. Balfour, has given a pledge that they are "desirous at the earliest possible opportunity to carry out on the mainland of the East Coast Protectorate what they have already carried out, or are in process of carrying out, upon the islands." The Government has also, through the Attorney-General, reaffirmed the law which previously existed, and which applies to runaway slaves, that "if a British subject detained a slave, it mattered not whether in a foreign country or on British territory, it was not in accordance with law."

One stipulation in the decrees of the Sultan Hamoud-bin-Mahomed-bin-Said requires consideration. Walis were appointed in the different districts of Zanzibar and Pemba, to whom every master or servant might appeal for justice "in respect of the alleged relations of master and slave." It was proposed by Lord Salisbury in his despatch that "British officials should be appointed to watch the cases and to prevent injustice." Seeing that the Arab Walis would naturally incline to favour the Arab masters, this proposal was essential to any satisfactory working of the Act. Joseph Albert Pease questioned Mr. Curzon in the House of Commons on the 28th May as to the appointment of these English officials, and received answer from the Under-Secretary that Mr. J. T. Last, F.R.G.S., of Chuaka, was appointed to watch all cases in the interior of the island of Zanzibar, while General Sir Lloyd William Mathews was to exercise supervision in the city, and that Mr. John Prediger Farler, of Tunduaua, would supervise all cases on

OUR RESIDENCE IN CHAKI-CHAKI.

H. Armitage, Photo.

the island of Pemba. These three men are probably the most efficient that could have been selected, and, from their previous experience, are well calculated to protect the negroes from injustice.

On Tuesday, the 6th April, 1897, the Arabs assembled at the Palace at Zanzibar to hear the decree. This day will long be a memorable one in the history of the islands. The Sultan first invited his brother and other members of his own family, to have the clauses read to them. Then he received fifty representative Arab sheikhs belonging to the island of Pemba, and subsequently sixty or seventy leading Arabs of the island of Zanzibar. Sir Lloyd Mathews, the Prime Minister, was the one European present. The Sultan advised the Arabs, on returning to their respective shambas, to adopt a conciliatory attitude towards their slaves, and to make them such concessions that the relations between employer and employed should be as little disturbed as possible. The Arab masters were encouraged by the Sultan to offer larger plots of land for the negroes to cultivate on their own account, and to arrange for them to have three days a week for cultivating their own plots, and give four days to their masters' service. It was hoped by some such arrangement to keep the negroes as much as possible on the shambas where they had been accustomed to work. The decrees were also posted up in Arabic at the residences of the Walis in Zanzibar and Pemba.

The news of the official proclamation spread in the city of Zanzibar, but no disturbance occurred, and for some days no slaves applied for their freedom. On shambas in outlying districts the slaves did not recognise any change. The Arabs were pleased to find that no sudden displacement was contemplated; they were gratified that their family life was not to be touched, and were agreeably surprised with the stipulation that they were to be compensated for the liberation of any slaves they legally held. In the course of the following few weeks some twenty-five slaves claimed the benefit of the decree and were liberated. Of their owners, twenty-one received compensation. The average compensation was £4 per head. Thirty-three slaves left for Arabia, a few were kidnapped, and others were taken across the sea. Fifteen runaways were given work as freemen at Dunga, and twenty at Tunduaua, on the Government shambas. Many Arabs listened to the advice of the Walis to make contracts with their slaves on the half-and-half principle, and thus kept them from running away. The change was working very slowly, the chief effect thus far being to make the masters more careful and indulgent, for fear of losing their men. Later on larger numbers of slaves came forward to the officials—from forty to sixty per month—and claimed their freedom. Some, both men and women, took advantage of their freedom, to wander about or to prostitute their acquired privileges. Many others came to endeavour to obtain more liberal terms from their old masters, electing to remain on easier terms where they had lived so long, asking for an extra day for themselves, or for an increased share of the crop. In not a few instances the attachment between master and servant was such that there was no disposition to change. But the negroes became more independent than hitherto, and the leaven of liberty was quietly working. Their condition, though remaining with their employers, has been ameliorated, and remarkably little friction has occurred. We hope more definite liberation will result hereafter.

CHAPTER XI.

EAST AFRICA PROTECTORATE.

"If you are going to stay in a place, build."—Swahili Proverb.

The East Africa Protectorate and Uganda are more absolutely under our own administration than Zanzibar and Pemba. The portion of the mainland which, by the arrangement of the 31st October, 1886, remained to the Sultan of Zanzibar, was the ten-miles strip from Wanga, at the mouth of the Umba, to Kipini, on the river Ozi. This territory was, unfortunately, not included in the scope of Lord Salisbury's despatch of February, 1897. The ten-miles strip does not embrace more than 170 miles of coast. The depth, however, is reckoned from high-water mark, so that near the creeks, and especially in the neighbourhood of Mombasa, the boundary is nearly twenty miles inland from the actual coast-line. The Sultan is also sovereign over the islands of Lamu, Manda, Patta, and Faga, and of the port and environs of Kismayu.

The Sultan's territory is held under what may be called a perpetual lease. He gets (or rather the Zanzibar Government gets) £17,000 a year for it, composed partly of the £11,000 a year which was paid to him by the old company, and partly of the interest (£6,000 a year) on the £200,000 (in consols) paid to him by Germany for the sale of his rights south of the Umba, and utilised with his consent by Her Majesty's late Government in order to buy out the Imperial British East Africa Company. He is considered sovereign of the country; his flag flies over the forts; and the Mohammedan religion and law are guaranteed as the established Church and legal system to the people of the ten-miles strip. Otherwise the administration is entirely British. There are native magistrates, called Walis, in the ten-miles strip, under the British District Officer. The Sultan occupies, in fact, something of the position of the Sultan of Turkey in Egypt. The Arabs prefer this arrangement to pure annexation, as, so long as they are under a " sovereign " of their own faith, the land is still " Dar-ut-Islam " and all that this implies, and they look on the red Arab flag much as an Australian or Canadian does on the Union Jack.

Within a stone's throw north-east of Kipini begins the Sultanate of Witu, which extends as far east as Kwyhoo, and the northern limit of which is a line running west from Kwyhoo, on the coast, to a point a few miles west of the Ozi river. The greatest depth of the Sultanate of Witu is about forty miles (near Kipini). Witu was under a German Protectorate till 1890, and was a terrible thorn in the side of the Sultans of Zanzibar and of the Imperial British East Africa Company. When Germany made over her Protectorate west of Kipini to us, she stipulated (Act 2 of the Anglo-German Agreement) for the maintenance of the Sultanate of Witu. The Sultanate is, however, rather nominal for all practical purposes, though under different names. Witu is a district of the province of Tanaland. The remainder of the coast to the north of Witu, as far as the river Juba, some 150 miles, was evacuated by the British East Africa Company on the 31st July, 1893, and the administration has been taken over by England. The Imperial British East Africa Company finally handed over the whole administration of the territories with which it was connected to the British Protectorate on the 1st July, 1895.

The territory to the south of the river Umba belongs to Germany, while north of the river Juba is under Italian influence. Our mainland Protectorate is administered direct from the Foreign Office in London, without reference to the Sultan. The officials are paid out of English revenue, and they hold their appointments under our Queen.

The coast is in a remarkable way dominated by the islands along its shore. The most important of these islands is Mombasa. A bridge, 1,732 feet long, now connects Mombasa with the mainland, and the town is one of rapidly increasing commercial importance, as well as being the centre of our East African Administration. It is connected by telegraph with Europe and India, and possesses the finest harbour in East Africa. The population is about 20,000. Approaching it from Europe, the old Portuguese fort is picturesque and conspicuous. The hospital stands high, and is prominent from the sea, and handsome European residences have recently been erected along the sea-front. We found Arab dhows lying alongside, full of camels, instead of the old cargoes of slaves. Men move briskly about the streets, with a new air of urgency, and the negro is gaining by association with English commerce. There is a strange mixture of old and new in the East African wine-skin. The iron pier, the steam crane, the English Customhouse, public notices in English in the market, with the names of the streets at the corners, all tell of the new spirit that is entering in. The water in the harbour lies quiet, with a gentle ripple, the waves being kept back by the long coral reef across the entrance of the bay. The fronds of the lofty

MOMBASA HARBOUR.

cocoanut palms wave languidly in the breeze on the shore to the north; the talipot palm and the green mango trees adorn the coral cliff; while a superabundance of tropical creepers hang over the rocky banks down to the water's edge. Mombasa presents an extraordinary field for ethnological study. Representatives of various African tribes are met in the streets, but there is a freedom of movement among the negroes that shows they are devoid of terror, and slavery in the ten-miles strip is not so severe as it has been in Pemba and Zanzibar.

Kilindini is a fine sheltered harbour on the west side of Mombasa island, and is available for large vessels. It is also a rising port. To the north of Malindi lie the three islands of Lamu, Manda, and Patta. The Arabs for many years contested the sovereignty of these islands with the Portuguese. Their sheltered waters form valuable harbours for commerce. The Arab traders fortified Patta, and lived there securely in their Oriental palaces. Here the arrogant Sultan Simba entrenched himself, and waxed strong. He was, however, compelled to fly, and Manda became a stronghold. The Gallas and the Swahili drove the Arabs out of Manda, and then the island of Lamu became their rendezvous. In 1507 the Portuguese Commander, Tristan da Cunha, captured Lamu, but had to yield it up again to Arab prowess. Now the islands and harbours enjoy the benign rule of Britannia. This coast-line must always to a large extent govern the commerce of the interior, and it is fortunate for England that she commands all the best harbours of East Africa.

As to the interior, the country up to the limits of the Congo Free State is divided into two Protectorates, with separate Commissioners and

Administrations. These are, first, the East African Protectorate, of which Mombasa is the capital, and of which Sir Arthur Hardinge is Administrator; and then the Uganda Protectorate. The East Africa Protectorate extends inland as far as the Kedong river, about 350 miles from Mombasa, its greatest width between Kismayu and the east border of the Uganda Protectorate being about 450 miles. It is divided into four Provinces, each of which has a Sub-Commissioner. The Provinces are sub-divided into Districts, each of which is governed by a Collector.* In organising these Districts the Government took as the basis of their sub-divisions geographical and ethnographical considerations, making Districts coincide as far as possible with tribal boundaries, so as to get the people of one tribe into one District. The Sultan's sovereignty is enshrined in the name of one Province, that of Mombasa, which, under the name of Seyyidieh, the "land of the Seyyid" (Seyyid, or Lord, being the name by which the Sultan is known to the people), includes nearly all the mainland portion of the Zanzibar territory.

The East Africa Protectorate not only embraces a most valuable coast-line, with excellent natural harbours and ports, but it also contains high tableland, which greatly modifies the climate of portions of the interior. This tableland has precipitous escarpments, and is in the neighbourhood of lofty

---

* The following are the Provinces and their Districts in our East Africa Protectorate :—

Province of SEYYIDIEH, including the Districts of Vanga, capital Wasin; Mombasa, capital Mombasa; and Malindi, capital Malindi.

Province of TANALAND, including the Districts of Tana River, capital Ngao; Lamu, capital Lamu; Port Durnford, capital Port Durnford; and Sultanate of Witu, capital Witu.

Province of JUBALAND, including the Districts of Lower Juba, capital Kismayu; Upper Juba, capital Malnugu-Kisungu; Ogaden, and Gusha.

Province of UKAMBA, including the Districts of Taita and Taveta, capital Ndi; Athi, capital Machakos; Kenia, capital Kikuyu; and Kitui, capital Kitui.

mountains. The Aberdare range is 14,000 feet high, while Mount Kenia rises 18,370 feet above the sea.

Though the Imperial British East Africa Company has now lapsed, it has a record on the anti-slavery question which ought not to be forgotten. Under the enlightened leadership of Sir William Mackinnon it did considerable towards the emancipation of slaves and protecting them from cruelty and injustice. The mainland presented far greater facilities for runaways than the islands. There is a common Swahili proverb which says, "*La watoro shaka n lili kwa lili*" ("The runaway slave always escapes to the nearest woods"). The runaways also often escaped to the nearest Mission stations, such as Freretown and Rabai. The Arabs became very restless and indignant at this, and in 1889 Colonel Euan Smith wrote to Lord Salisbury that the storm of indignation was rising, so that these two stations "would inevitably become the object of attack before many months were over." This unsettlement was partly caused by the disturbances in the German sphere of influence. However, Sir Euan Smith's alarm was fortunately allayed by the wise administration of Mr. George S. Mackenzie. The legal right of the owner to the slaves having been established by the Mohammedan power, and recognised by Great Britain, Mr. Mackenzie agreed to pay a fixed sum of twenty-five dollars for each fugitive found at the Missions, on receiving which the owners consented to grant freedom papers to the slaves. Five hundred and fifty of these slaves belonged to tribes in the interior; and as no means offered of getting them safely back to their old homes without being recaptured, "permits of residence" were granted to them, authorising them to remain at the Mission stations. The payment amounted to a gross sum of £3,500, which was subscribed from various sources. The ceremony of the presentation of the free papers took place at the Church Missionary Society station at Rabai, on the 1st January, 1889, amid a great concourse of Arabs and of the native population. Such a scene had seldom before been witnessed in Africa. The Arabs were conciliated, the Mission stations were saved from attack, and 1,422 slaves were set free. General L. W. Mathews and Mr. George S. Mackenzie presided over the presentation to the negroes, and a triumphal trophy of palm branches and other decorations was erected by the people in honour of the festive occasion. Two hundred and twenty-three others were liberated on the ten-miles strip by working out the cost of freedom by their own industry, 81 were freed by their owners, and 201 obtained freedom under the decree of 1st August, 1890, in consequence of their owners dying without lawful children. The total number thus obtaining freedom during the Company's administration was therefore 2,387.*

Another centre of a different character in the East Africa Protectorate is at Gusha, on the river Juba. Many slaves who were discontented escaped beyond the ten-miles strip to Gusha, and thousands of negroes established themselves there, under their own so-called Sultans. The negro slaves on the ten-miles strip were not, as a rule, unkindly treated, but they were sorely grieved at the way in which the Arabs snatched their daughters from them, and appropriated them to their own harems. The Arab masters live in the coast towns with their household slaves, while on an inland estate, or somewhere along the shore-line, they may have 200 or 300 slaves

* McDermott's "East Africa," page 221.

working for them under a native overseer, who is himself a slave. The Arab probably visits his estate twice a year to receive the produce. He is honoured on such visits with much palaver and tamasha, and returns to his house in town. The overseer has a large house in the centre of the estate, the slaves have their huts on the same property, with their garden allotment, which the wife and the man cultivate on Thursdays and Fridays; or if the man lives on the shore he often fishes for his sustenance. The tall grass and thick brushwood grow between the slave's hut and the neighbouring houses on the estate, and the man is left a good deal to his own devices, as long as he works five days a week for his master. Sometimes he carries a gun for defence from animals, his master providing the equipment.

Captain Dundas describes the valley of the Juba river as very fertile, and the district of Gusha for eighty miles as being "one long plantation of sem-sem, maize, millet, plantain, tobacco, and cotton." The river is about 100 yards wide. Tall palms and luxuriant vegetation clothe its banks with beauty. Zebras and antelopes abound. The citizens are on excellent terms with the English, and the Government stern-wheeler comes up the river every year. The steamer, on arriving at Gusha, picks up a number of men as free labourers. A dozen American axes from the steamer's stores are handed out to them to chop wood for fuel. The people turn out in crowds to cheer the steamer as it passes; and the town, with its environs, is becoming an important centre of new life.

The fearless protest of Bishop Tucker against the omission of the mainland from the privileges of the decree of 6th April, 1897, with regard to the abolition of the legal status of slavery, has brought prominently before the House of Commons the question of further emancipation. Bishop Tucker wrote urgently to *The Times* on the 12th April, impeaching the despatch of Lord Salisbury as being unsatisfactory on three counts: first, that it continued many of the women of Zanzibar and Pemba in slavery; secondly, that it only provided a "limited freedom" for the male slaves, with compensation to the master; and thirdly, that it excluded the Mombasa portion of the Sultanate from the operation of the Government proposals. On the 21st May, 1897, a conference of members of Parliament and of anti-slavery advocates was held in a committee-room of the House of Commons. The Right Hon. Sir John Kennaway presided, and Bishop Tucker gave evidence. The conference resulted in questions being put in the House of Commons to the Foreign Under-Secretary by Joseph Albert Pease and others. In the course of the discussion that followed in reference to the action of British officials at Mombasa requiring that runaway slaves should be delivered up to them by the missionaries, the Attorney-General declared that it "is unlawful for a British subject to detain a slave, whether in a foreign country or on British territory." Mr. Curzon stated on the 28th June that a telegram had been sent to the Commissioner at Mombasa informing him that a British subject is breaking the law if he takes part in restoring to his master, or otherwise deprives of his liberty, any fugitive slave, and instructing the Commissioner to conform his conduct to the law thus laid down. The hunting up of runaway slaves by authority of British officials, such as had been done at Rabai and elsewhere in the neighbourhood of Mombasa, has thus been stopped. It is only fair to the Arabs and to the local authorities to remember that the hunting up of runaways was alleged often

UGANDA RAILWAY, KILINDINI, MOMBASA.

to be undertaken because the slaves had escaped to evade the just penalty of crimes they had committed. In common English law, however, no magistrate issues a summons for the arrest of any man without stating on such summons the charge that is laid against him. In the papers for arresting runaways which were produced in the House of Commons there was no crime stated or laid to the charge of these runaways, and the papers and arrest by English officials or their subordinates were illegal. The action of the House of Commons went further, and the Right Hon. A. J. Balfour, on the 24th June, assured members that " the Government are earnestly desirous at the earliest possible opportunity to carry out on the mainland of the East Coast Protectorate what they had already carried out, or were in the process of carrying out, upon the islands."

Thus two important points were gained with regard to future action tending towards emancipation on the mainland. But it is always necessary for reformers at home to remember the words of Lieutenant C. S. Smith, late Vice-Consul at Zanzibar, on the limitations that should moderate our expectations : " Unfortunately, the enactment of a law or the ratification of a treaty in the capital does not necessarily involve obedience in the corners of the world, least of all from such persons as are likely to turn their hands to slave-trading."[*] We sometimes get excellent resolutions and decrees on paper, with Government authority, but it may take years ere their effects percolate through the inertia of tropical populations, environed with the customs of centuries, in vast territories, parts of which have never yet been explored by Englishmen,

---

[*] Chapter on Slavery, pages 375-432, by Lieutenant C. S. Smith, in " History of the Universities' Mission."

territories untraversed by railways or telegraphs, where no newspapers enlighten, where no administration is locally established, and where the most intelligent part of the population may consider that the decree, if it does reach them, conflicts with their own interests.

The legal status of slavery in the East Africa Protectorate only exists in the ten-miles strip and adjacent islands and in Witu, where the Zanzibar laws on the subject were introduced. Kismayu, however, is an exception, slavery having been abolished there by Seyyid Burghash. The abolition was not very real until the English Government took over the administration in 1895. The domestic slaves at Kismayu appear seldom to have applied for freedom, though they can get it for asking. There may be about 26,000 slaves altogether in this District of Seyyidieh, which our Government holds on lease from the Sultan of Zanzibar. Many of them were sold by their parents during the famine thirteen years ago.

Uganda* now constitutes a separate Protectorate, and promises to be a most important factor in Central African civilisation. Its eastern frontier runs parallel with the East Africa Protectorate. To the west it runs right up to the Congo Free State. Southwards it abuts the German Protectorate, while its north-west limits remain undefined. The present Commissioner of Uganda is Mr. Berkeley.

The geographical features of this inland Protectorate indicate a remarkable commercial future, while it is virtually the key to the whole of the Nile valley, and commands its trade from the south. Great Britain, in holding Uganda, can therefore, to a large extent, annihilate the slave trade that

* The Uganda Districts, from south-east to north-west, are: Masai, Kavirondo, Usoga, Uganda proper, Buddu, Toru, and Unyoro.

passed northwards from Central Africa up the Nile valley, and at the same time can tap regions whose trade, as civilisation extends, must greatly increase, and be of permanent value to our commerce.

The tablelands of Uganda promise to be the future home of many an English emigrant, the temperature usually varying from 60° to 80°, occasionally rising to 90° or falling to 55°. Rain is very frequent, but the mean annual rainfall does not exceed fifty to sixty inches. The country contains many lofty mountains. Mfumbiro is 10,000 feet high, Mount Eglon is 14,100 feet, and Ruwenzori is 16,600 feet. The vast Lake Victoria Nyanza is 3,900 feet above the Indian Ocean. It is 150 miles across, and 200 miles long. The equator runs for 400 miles through this promising Protectorate, which has undoubtedly a magnificent future before it, being adapted for all kinds of tropical culture.

In the past, the porterage system has given a great impetus to slave-raiding and to the slave trade. The captives brought quantities of ivory down to the coast, while cotton and European fabrics were carried up to the interior on the heads of slave porters. The railway from Mombasa to the Victoria Nyanza will, it is hoped, prove a great anti-slavery agency. Our Government, after many hesitations, happily undertook its construction in 1895. It is to be 660 miles long, and the first hundred miles are already open, and trains running upon it. The issue of £3,000,000 from consols was authorised for its construction. When this great route is once completed, the perils from fever during the journey up country will be minimised, and the future of Uganda assured. The Protectorate was proclaimed on the 19th June, 1894, and included the country then subject to King Mwanga. In 1896 the administration was extended to Unyoro and

Usoga. In 1897 King Mwanga rebelled and fled. He had been guilty, in November, 1896, of trying to smuggle 2,000 pounds weight of ivory. He was consequently visited with restrictions and warned. Buddu was the Province secured to the Roman Catholics in the political settlement by the late Sir Gerald Portal in 1893, and became a centre for plots against the English Administration. On the 27th August, 1897, telegrams arrived in England announcing that an insurrection in Buddu had been quelled, and that Mwanga had escaped across the German frontier. When he fled to the Germans he was taken by them to Bukoba; and although he had 400 lads with him, the Germans only allowed ten to remain, and arranged for him to go on to Mwanza.

On the 14th August, Daudi Chwa, the son of Mwanga, was proclaimed King of Uganda, at Nakasero, in the room of his father. He was just one year old. Daudi was then taken to Mengo, and at the main gateway was set on his throne, robed in a bark-cloth. Two spears and a shield were held over him, and he was declared to have "eaten" Uganda. The little princess, Yunia Kamwanda, daughter of Kalema, was proclaimed to be the Queen sister, and was also robed in bark-cloth. Apolo Kagwe, Mugwania, and the Kangao were appointed the three Regents to administer the government in the name of Daudi until he is old enough to do so himself. The cause of the rebellion does not appear to have been any harshness shown by Europeans. Mr. R. H. Leakey says that the presence of the missionaries saved the adjoining Province of Koki, the native Christians there remaining loyal to a man.

The mutiny of Soudanese troops in Usoga in October, 1897, accompanied with serious loss of life, shows the peril of leaning on native armed forces in such a remote district. Major Macdonald, on his route to Lake Rudolph, appears to have had with him one of the largest caravans that had ever been known in that part of Africa. Such disturbances naturally awaken distrust in the neighbouring provinces.

Through the energy of the Church Missionary Society, Uganda has become a centre of light, dispelling slavery by the dynamic force of Christian teaching. Reformation obviates revolution. Christianity is the real antidote for slavery. Change of heart is more effectual than edicts of Sultans or votes of Parliament. The anti-slavery movement in Uganda is based on the dissemination of Gospel truth. For the last four or five years the Uganda Mission has stood as an advanced bulwark in the heart of Africa. In March, 1893, a slave ran away from his Mohammedan taskmaster, and found a hiding-place with a Christian chief of the name of Bartolemayo. The Arab demanded his surrender. The native Christians said it was contrary to their consciences to surrender slaves. Bishop Tucker was appealed to, and replied that so long as slavery was the law of the land they must respect the law of their King, and that the right course was by constitutional methods to try to get the law changed. The Bishop referred them to the story of Philemon and Onesimus, and told the native Christians to pray about it and to search the Scriptures and confer among themselves as to their duty. In due course the following remarkable paper was handed in, bearing the signatures of forty Protestant chiefs:—" All we Protestant chiefs wish to adopt these good customs of freedom. We agree to untie and free completely all our slaves. Here are our names as chiefs."

Perhaps no more magnificent testimony could be given to the vital force of Christian truth, and to the genuine work of the Church Missionary Society, than such a document, coming without suggestion from forty African chiefs, with no compulsion save the constraining love of Christ. "It is," says Bishop Tucker, "perhaps the most significant event recorded in the modern history of the continent of Africa, and will rejoice the hearts of all who inherit the work and traditions of the Buxtons, the Wilberforces, and all who have laboured in the cause of freedom for the slave. It is nothing less than a declaration of the desire of the majority of the great chiefs in Uganda that slavery should be entirely abolished." Within the jurisdiction of these chiefs there will be no more bartering of men, women, and children, like so many cattle. One of the great incentives of war is thus removed. For generations in Africa tribe has waged war against tribe, in the hope of capturing slaves. The influence of a strong English Government, accompanied by earnest evangelistic work on the part of missionaries at the sources of the Nile, can scarcely be overestimated in its bearings on the future of Africa. A strategic position of immense value is thus growing in moral and material strength year by year.

CHURCH MISSIONARY HOUSE, FRERETOWN.

CHAPTER XII.

EXISTING MISSIONARY WORK.

"The worker of success in matters is God."—*Swahili Proverb.*

MISSIONARY work in East Africa dates from 1844, when John Ludwig Krapf landed on the 3rd January, at Mombasa. He visited Zanzibar, where he received a letter from Seyyid Saïd, to the following effect: "This letter is written on behalf of Dr. Krapf, the German good man who wishes to convert the world to God." Within two months of his settlement at Mombasa, he buried his wife and child on the mainland where Freretown now stands. He wrote home:—"Tell our friends that there is, on the East African coast, a lonely grave of a member of the Mission cause connected with your Society. This is a sign that you have commenced the struggle with this part of the world; and as the victories of the Church are gained by stepping over the graves and death of many of her members, you may be the more convinced that the hour is at hand when you are summoned to the conversion of Africa from its eastern shore."[*] In 1846 John Rebmann joined his fellow-countryman, and thus was founded the work of the Church Missionary Society in East Africa, which in Uganda has blossomed as the rose. Krapf and Rebmann established the Mission at Kisulutini, in the Rabai District, and the latter remained twenty-nine years in East Africa without coming home. When Sir Bartle Frere visited the Mission

[*] "Church Missionary Atlas," eighth edition, page 48.

in 1873 he found Rebmann perfectly blind, immersed in his dictionaries, translating with the help of his faithful native attendant, Isaac Nyondo. When Sir Bartle Frere returned home in 1873 he urged the Church Missionary Society to form a settlement for liberted slaves, and this resulted in the foundation of Freretown in 1874. Thus were formed the Mission stations of Mombasa, Freretown, and Rabai, besides other centres of the Church Missionary Society in the interior. The United Methodist Free Churches have also a good Mission at Ribe.

On our arrival in Mombasa we at once visited the Rev. F. Burt, who kindly acted as our guide to the Bible Society's House, to the Ladies' Mission, and to the Boys' School. Thence we proceeded to the Medical Mission at Mzizima, where we had the pleasure of meeting Dr. Edwards and his wife. The hospital work is accomplished by the segregation of different diseases in various small houses, rather than by crowding patients in one large establishment. The exquisitely situated property, with its abundant tropical foliage, lends itself to this system, affording from the ridge charming views across the bay. Dr. Edwards was formerly a civil engineer, but finding that the Missionary Society did not then want an engineer, and feeling called to the work, he qualified for a doctor.

Through groves of custard apples and oleanders we made our way down a rocky path to the shore, and found a naughty man who has charge of the ferry, saying his prayers. He blesses God and curses his fellow-men. We sat on the ground under a palm, waiting his leisure, and then, while Mr. Burt reminded this ferry official that out of the same mouth ought not to proceed blessing and cursing, we dragged a wretched old "dugout," made from the trunk of a baobab tree, to the water's edge, and got into it. I confess I did not feel very safe, but had confidence in our good guide, and thus we floated across from Mombasa island to the mainland, and were soon in Freretown. We passed the little shanty, with its palm-leaf roof, in which the good Bishop of Equatorial Africa holds farewell prayer-meetings with his fellow-missionaries before starting for Uganda; and we admired the Oriental surroundings and simplicity of Christian life which the scene betokened. Passing through an avenue of stately mangoes, planted by the Portuguese long ago, we were met by a group of English ladies returning from their mid-day prayer-meeting, and soon reached the central Mission House, where the Rev. H. K. Binns gave us a cordial welcome. He went to Freretown in 1876, and has had some twenty years' experience of Mission work among the freed men. Four Swahili spears adorned the wall of his dining-room, with the words enscrolled upon them, "*Heri walio safi mioyo kwani watamwona muungu*" (Matt. v. 8). The brilliant scarlet flowers of the African acacia hung in clusters from the trees outside the verandah, while bright convolvuluses and other creepers scaled the walls. The views of Mombasa harbour from the upper balcony of the Mission House are exquisite.

Some 700 or 800 people live in this Christian village. Many of them have their huts distributed about on the property, surrounded with plots under their own cultivation. A large town bell calls them to public gatherings and to prayers, and we watched them in their market, chaffering in Swahili for vegetables, fruit, fish, and cotton goods. The freed people, men and women, look well-favoured, their well-rounded limbs betokening a sufficiency of food. Not a few of them are quite stout, and the Christian village bears the impress of the sheltering care of philanthropists, rather than of the hard struggle for existence that faces men in the keen competition of the world. When we reflect for a moment on the degradation from which many of these people have been delivered, we cannot but rejoice in their deliverance and in the safeguarding they enjoy. For calling out the energy of life that is begotten of conflict, it is probably better that Christian converts should mingle in the ordinary traffic of men rather than be secluded on compounds. In the *transition* from slavery to freedom, from dependence to independence, such centres as Freretown are invaluable refuges, and will be useful for a long time to come as centres from which life and light radiate. We visited the church, with its well-furnished interior and solid teakwood seats. The transept is spanned in the form of a rainbow above the audience, with the golden words, " *Watamwita jina lakwe IMANUELI mngu pamoja nashwi* " (the latter clause of Matt. i. 23).

We had much converse with the Rev. Harry K. Binns respecting slavery and emancipation. From his large experience his judgment is very valuable. Like all other missionaries, he longs for emancipation. He is, nevertheless, aware of the difficulties which surround progress. His views contain much food for thought with regard to future action, and it is better to give his own words rather than any summary of them. He says :—" The whole of my life spent in Africa has been one long fight on behalf of the slave : first to save him from his master, and secondly to save him from himself. I have stood between the master and his slave—not always to protect the slave. I remember once throwing my arms round an Arab slave-owner, and having his blood run down my clothes, in order to protect him from runaway slaves. Good slaves, as a rule, do not run away from their masters, unless the latter are more than usually cruel. The slaves generally run away from one of three causes—either they have committed a theft and feared the consequences; or they were lazy and their masters threatened to punish them; or there was a woman in the case, such as a slave running away with another man's wife, or a slave running away with his own wife because he feared she would be taken from him; but I hardly ever came across a case of a slave having been cruelly beaten, although I have heard of cases."* The conversation turned on the necessity, in the event of emancipation, of making provision for the infirm and aged, and for controlling the younger portion of the population, to save them from vagrancy, idleness, and prostitution. On the latter of these points Mr. Binns feels strongly. He says:—"The most important point of all I believe to be that in regard to the rising generation. The whole of the youthful population, many of whom are fatherless and motherless, and would be, if emancipated, masterless and homeless as well, should be taken off the streets of the coast towns and placed under control—educated, too, but I fear this is too much to expect, unless the Missionary Societies undertake it. I was speaking to a Government official of high standing, not long ago, and he told me that he considered it a great mistake to educate the African, that they were much more easily governed if left ignorant heathen, that cheap education was the curse of India, &c. I do not, however, believe that these opinions are held by Government officials in general, or by the English nation at large. I am hoping, therefore, that when the Government decide upon the abolition of slavery, they will also decide

* *Church Missionary Intelligencer*, June, 1897, page 462.

CITY OF ZANZIBAR, FROM THE SHAMBA.

upon some liberal plan by which the slave may be controlled, educated, and raised in the social scale, and I am convinced that the Missionary Societies will do their utmost to place within the reach of all that everlasting Gospel of the grace of God which alone can truly raise the slave here, and make him fit for glory hereafter."* It is probably more than we can at present expect from any Government that a system of elementary education should be established in the African Protectorates such as we have inaugurated in India. This may be the programme of the future. Meanwhile, the urgency of guarding the young freed people to which Mr. Binns refers must engage the attention of every Missionary Society working in Africa.

The Universities' Mission has its headquarters in Zanzibar. In Central Africa, as well as in the island, much earnest educational work is going forward, as well as the direct preaching of the Gospel. We visited the Cathedral and the various mission agencies that cluster round it; we also went to Kiungani and Mbweni. The origin of the Mission in 1859 dates from the thrilling addresses of Dr. Livingstone when he was in England in 1857. Many of us remember hearing him during that memorable visit. His own soul was kindled by that growing missionary fire which often begins in quiet hours of conviction in home lands, but which is fanned into a flame by the experience of actual contact with heathenism, and which burns with quickened zeal in the riper experiences of matured work. On the 4th December, 1857, Livingstone addressed the students in Cambridge. His reception was enthusiastic and inspiring. He also appealed to the undergraduates at Oxford. His parting words rang in the ears of both

* *Church Missionary Intelligencer*, June, 1897, page 462.

Universities: "I go back to Africa to try to make an open path for commerce and Christianity. Do you carry out the work which I have begun. *I leave it with you.*" Under such heroic impulses the Universities' Mission was founded. The scope of its operations is stated clearly in its Constitution: "Its object is the establishment and maintenance of stations in Central Africa, which may serve as centres of Christianity and civilisation, for the promotion of true religion, and the ultimate extinction of the slave trade. In order to accomplish these designs, the plan of the Mission is to maintain, under the government of bishops, both bodies of clergy and lay-helpers, including medical men and artificers, European or African, capable of conducting the work of building and husbandry."*

Preliminary efforts were made to form the headquarters on the mainland, but on the 31st August, 1864, Bishop Tozer and Dr. Steere landed in Zanzibar, and proceeded to establish the Mission in that city. It was a happy selection, and was, without doubt, the pointing of Divine providence. The island of Zanzibar was the strategic key of the position if the Universities' Mission was to organise stations in the interior. Its growth in Zanzibar and on the mainland may be guaged from the fact that since 1860 no fewer than 290 English ladies and gentlemen have gone out to their appointed stations. Of these, up to the close of 1896, sixty-six died in the service, ninety-seven had "withdrawn," and forty-two others had been "invalided" home. These facts show that there is much which missionaries and missionary committees have to struggle against with regard to health and conditions of work in Central Africa. They show how important it is to investigate the qualifications, physical constitution,

* "History of Universities' Mission," page 434.

and temperament of candidates before they go out, and to make adequate provision on the spot for the maintenance of health.

The Cathedral of the Universities' Mission, known as Christ Church, stands on the site of the old slave market. It is a remarkable structure, and is a monument of the perseverance and industry of Bishop Steere. In 1873 Dr. Steere was able to chronicle, in the joy of his heart, "The last open slave market in the world has been closed." The site was presented to him as a free gift by a Hindu merchant, Jairam Senji. The following year Dr. Steere was consecrated Bishop in Westminster Abbey. On his return to Zanzibar he devoted himself to the erection of Christ Church, which was opened in 1879. The roof is an evidence of the Bishop's boldness and skill. Wood could not be used because of the white ants, nor iron because of the heat of the sun. He therefore resolved to build it of concrete over wooden supports, which were afterwards removed. The span of arched concrete forming the roof is twenty-eight and a-half feet! The centre-line is sixty feet above the pavement. It still stands solid. Mr. Charles W. Roberts, who resides in the Mission House, kindly took me to the Cathedral. He has fifty or sixty young men under his care, and some 200 to 300 people in the city are connected with the Mission. Mr. Roberts has been in East Africa for sixteen years, and is in capital health. Reasonable care, precaution, and self-control constitute his philosophy of life in the tropics. Adjoining the Mission is the Hospital, with trained nurses; and close by is the Mission Printing Office, where three Europeans were working with young native printers at old-fashioned presses. The effort deserves new machines and equipment. Other industrial departments are being developed. Schools and zenana work are carried on in the neighbourhood. For twenty years the central Mission House, Mkunazini, stood here, but in 1895 it was pulled down.

At Kiungani I had the privilege of meeting the late Archdeacon P. L. Jones-Bateman. He then seemed in vigorous health, but has since succumbed to the climate, and thus another valuable life has passed away. He welcomed me in the library, which is a treasure-house of books for a missionary in a foreign land. He was preparing a number of native young men "for holy orders." The truth is, Kiungani abounds with young men, and I found them enjoying football in thoroughly boyish fashion. The estate was purchased by Bishop Tozer in 1864, with funds provided by men belonging to the Wells Theological College in England. It therefore seems fitting that, with such an origin, a college for training Christian natives for Mission work should stand on Kiungani. The church and other buildings are erected on the spur of a hill looking out on the sea towards the mountains on the mainland, where some of these young men may hereafter be located, at Magila or other centres belonging to the Universities' Mission. There are about 120 boys and young men in the establishment, thirty of whom are liberated slaves. Unfortunately, low lagoons lie on both sides of the hill, and make the locality malarial.

Theodore Burtt and I, in company with Vice-Consul Kestell-Cornish, visited Mbweni. This shamba was intended for girls who had been liberated from slavery, or captured from slave dhows and handed over to the Mission. But as the slave trade is now practically at an end in the Protectorate, the house will be open for other native children. Miss Alice Foxley kindly showed us the premises. A group of her girls saluted her with delight, and almost with cheers, as she appeared at the main entrance. She had been absent for a few days, invalided. She caught hold of one little black child and drew her close to her side, saying to us, "This girl was pulled out of the bottom of a dhow in 1896, and handed over to us by the Government." The British and Foreign Bible Society's version of the Old Testament in Swahili is in high favour at Mbweni. The children greatly appreciate its Orientalisms. The story of the coming out of Egypt appeals to slave girls far more vividly than it can appeal to the freeborn children of England. There are eighty children in the house, and forty day scholars from the surrounding parish. The Industrial Department is an African gem. The girls take in washing from the neighbours; they also make good mats for flooring. They dye the grass different colours, and then plait the mat, blending the colours in neat patterns. Adjoining this shamba is the charming residence of Miss C. D. M. Thackeray. For the last twenty years she has given herself to the rescue of native girls. Sir John Kirk formerly resided on this shamba, and it abounds with beautiful tropical shrubs and palms. The old tennis-court remains as Sir John Kirk left it years ago. Miss Thackeray has all the enthusiasm of youth in her work, and her house is crowded with negro children. They look up to her as to a mother, and she maintains her interest in them in after years.

One of the most charming features of Mbweni is the Christian Village for freed men and women. They live in huts on both sides of the road, surrounded with their garden plots. There are some 140 of these people. We found them, in the cool of the evening, sitting and lying about under their own palm trees and oleanders, while the curly-headed, round-faced children and the chickens tumbled out from under the bananas and tall ferns to see us pass. These allotments, tenanted with such contented, well-favoured natives, none daring to make them afraid, form a striking contrast to the strange stories of cruel wrong which many of them can tell of the dark days of slave-raiding.

While the Universities' Mission is doing good work of many kinds in different centres in and around Zanzibar, we were glad to find that English sailors are not neglected. For these and for others there is the Strangers' Rest in Zanzibar, in which Captain and Mrs. Agnew are much interested. Mr. and Mrs. Knapman live at the Rest, the former visiting the sailors on board the ships and in other ways, and both are zealously engaged in promoting evangelical faith. While the Universities' Mission, with its many agencies, is a zealous observer of religious ceremonial and priestly orders, the Strangers' Rest, in lowlier guise, maintains great simplicity in its free Gospel services. Both are means for good; and having been in daily contact with boys as our servants, who had been trained in the Universities' Mission, I can speak favourably of their reverent participation in our devotional gatherings, and of the cheerful way in which they willingly rendered household service.

The French Catholics are building a large church in Zanzibar, and are active. The French Hospital is a great boon, and is very efficient.

The accummulating experience of these various Missionary Societies points to the wisdom of adapting varied means in the attainment of the varied ends aimed at. While the prime aim must ever be the proclamation of the Gospel of salvation through our Lord Jesus Christ, this aim by no

CATHEDRAL OF UNIVERSITIES' MISSION, ZANZIBAR.

means excludes medical missions, educational effort, and industrial work. If the lines of broad Christian statesmanship are observed in the elevation of native races, there will be no tendency to exalt one means to the depreciation of others. Each has its own appropriate place, and a well-equipped Mission may include all four agencies. There is probably no hesitation on the part of anyone in affirming the need for direct evangelistic teaching, or for medical and educational work, but it may be well to cite evidence with regard to the special need in Africa for Industrial Missions. The fact that slaves have been accustomed to work under compulsion, and that almost every kind of manual employment is, unfortunately, connected in their minds with slavery, makes it very needful to practically teach them the dignity of labour and the utter unprofitableness of idleness.

Sir Bartle Frere, as the result of his own observation in Africa, says :—" If I might presume to advise missionaries, I would introduce a far larger industrial element into their schools. Everyone should learn a trade, a mechanical art of some kind, or sufficient of agriculture to support himself. The teaching might be such as a good native artisan, or mechanic, or cultivator could impart, to which might be added, tentatively and with caution, instruction in European methods and the use of European tools, which are not invariably adapted to African habits and necessities. Every boy should, I think, be taught to make himself useful in building a hut, in cultivating, in managing a boat, in mending his own clothes and shoes, and nets and fishing tackle, after the native fashion, with European improvements only when clearly seen to be better than native ways."*

* "Eastern Africa," Sir Bartle Frere, pages 95, 96.

A. M. Mackay, with all his zeal for Christ and for soul-winning, expressed himself strongly on the advantages that modern scientific skill and appliances were able to render to Christian Missions, and justly says :—" To make use of means does not necessarily mean to rely on the means, though some cry out about an arm of flesh ; while they themselves are every day of their lives enjoying untold benefits from the presence of that arm. Labour without prayer is vain, but prayer without labour is sloth." " Mechanical work is probably as legitimate an aid to Missions as medical; nor do I see why one should not be as helpful to missionary work as the other, except for the difficulty of getting out of the rut our ideas run in."*

Major Lugard remarks :—" The value of the Industrial Mission can hardly be over-estimated among such people as the Waganda, both on account of their natural aptitude and their eager desire to learn. But even the less-advanced and more primitive tribes may be equally benefited if not only mechanical and artisan work, such as the carpenter's and blacksmith's craft, but also the simpler expedients of agriculture are taught."† Respecting the disposal of slaves when they are freed, and have nowhere to work, he says :— " It can best be effected by placing them either in colonies, under the supervision of a European, or in *Industrial* Missions. I think no better plan for the good of the natives exists than Industrial Missions. They might become not merely centres for educating the natives of the district in useful crafts, but small colonies of liberated slaves as well."‡ " Beyond doubt, I think the most useful Missions are the

---

* " Mackay of Uganda," pages 251 and 286.
† " Rise of our East African Empire," page 70.
‡ *Ibid*, pages 189, 190.

medical and the industrial, in the initial stages of savage development."*

Lovedale presents a practical working out of this principle of adapting varied means for the achievement of the one great end. James Stewart speaks of what he calls the Lovedale method. He says:—"Practical work must be combined with religious teaching. A good Christian should be a good workman up to the point of his natural ability, and as far as his moral sense has been developed and informed. The religion of the African, however, tends to be more or less emotional."† There is thus needed "truth and reality in work as well as in word."

Mr. Sharpe, of Nyasa, writes warmly of the excellent work done by the missionaries on their coffee plantations at Blantyre, in the Shirè highlands, and says:—"This district offers an object-lesson to all who doubt the native African's capacity for work. The settlement is now some twenty years old, and has passed beyond the experimental stage. Natives are quick to follow a lead when they see it brings them profit. Quite a number of Blantyre natives have now accounts at the local bank. The African is not a fool in such matters; he is able to look after his own interests, and is not so easily imposed on as is sometimes supposed."‡

These witnesses from various centres of action all confirm the judgment that Industrial Missions have an important part to play among other agencies in raising Africa to its appropriate place in the destiny of nations, and that good work may be quite as powerful a witness to the Gospel as good words.

---

* "Rise of our East African Empire," page 69.
† "Lovedale, South Africa," page 9.
‡ *Geographical Journal* for April, 1896.

CHAPTER XIII.

FRIENDS' INDUSTRIAL MISSION, BANANI.

"To him that is gracious to his neighbour, God is gracious."
Swahili Proverb.

No adequate mandate or justification for the establishment of a Christian Mission exists except the call of God. The responsibilities and the risks to human life in the tropics are so great that no Society can legitimately send out labourers unless God requires it. But the bond of universal brotherhood and of human need, combined with outward providences, are links in the chain that ratify and enforce the call. We have seen in the previous chapter the varied lines of service in which missionaries are employed in East Africa. The Society of Friends was already actively engaged in Missions in Madagascar, India, Ceylon, Syria, China, Turkey, and Bulgaria. The Missionary Committees of the Society in London were already responsible for seventy-five missionaries at work in those fields. It is, therefore, necessary to recount the way in which God seemed to be leading forth the Society into further work in Africa. Two Friends had been engaged in Mission work among the Zulus since 1879. The cause of the slave had rested upon the heart of the community for generations. For two centuries the negro had obtained the sympathy of the Friends' Church, and in America many lives had been consecrated to lifting the coloured people into the privileges of freedom and of citizenship. The Gurneys, the Forsters, the Sturges, the

DIGGING FOUNDATIONS OF MISSION HOUSE AT BANANI.
H. Armitage, Photo.

Harveys, and the Allens in England, and John G. Whittier, John Woolman, Levi Coffin, Elizabeth L. Comstock, Francis T. King, and a host of other worthies in America had fought the peaceable battle for emancipation. The cause of the slave had thus become the chosen inheritance of a people who believed that in the Fatherhood of God and the brotherhood of man every human being was an object of their fraternal regard. In the House of Commons, John Bright, William Edward Forster, Joseph Pease, and other Friends and descendants of Friends in the last generation had advocated the rights of man, as man, to the common privileges of liberty. From time to time the Spirit of God had moved Friends to practical work for the non-combatants in France, for distress in Bulgaria, for the persecuted Stundists in Russia, for the Armenians in Turkey. Then came that strange partition of Africa to which reference has frequently been made in these pages, and the conscience of the Christian Churches of England awoke to the fact that while it had been our national boast for a generation that when a slave touched our shores in any part of this great Empire that moment he was free, we had, almost without consideration of all that it involved, assumed the Protectorate of millions of souls in Africa, and tens of thousands of slaves. At the peril of their lives, year after year, before the American Civil War, slaves had tracked northward from the States through snow and flood, across prairie and ice, knowing that if they could but once cross our frontier into Canada and shelter under the Union Jack they were free. And now philanthropists held down their heads for shame as they heard of the horrors of slavery still perpetrated in our Protectorates in Africa. The Friends, among many others, pleaded that slavery must no longer be tolerated there. And in some ways the conscience of England and of Europe was more outspoken on the subject than it had been a generation before. The Brussels Conference of 1876, the Berlin Conference of 1884-5, and the Brussels Slave Trade Congress of 1889-90 took international ground on the question of slavery, which was an honour to every nation concerned, and by mutual agreement the signatories determined to do their part for the extinction of the slave trade. But it was a difficult work, and not to be done in a day. Step by step the movement has advanced, but much remains yet to be done. The enfranchisement of Africa was a great undertaking even for Europe. Japheth, however, in his own peculiar way, by process of occupation, set forth to emancipate the tents of Ham.

The Christian Church could not sit still in the presence of one of the most unique and one of the most gigantic movements that had ever been attempted in the history of the world—the conversion of a continent. Moffat and Livingstone sounded their clarion call to the battle for the uplifting of the negro race. Hannington, Mackay, and a host of other soldiers of the Cross fell on the hot fields of Africa, martyrs for Christ and for the brotherhood of nations. Every religious and secular paper was discussing African interests, and offering solutions for African problems. On the 28th December, 1895, *The Spectator* took up the old theme, and declared its philanthropic tendencies in the following words :—" The negro is the ' little sweep' of the human race, and we have no feeling towards him except a kindly pity for the suffering which he has usually undergone at its hands. We contend that the negro, though as deserving of consideration as any other race, fully entitled to justice, to freedom, and to as much happiness as it can obtain, is of all races the least hopeful, the one which has displayed least of the distinctive human power of accumulating knowledge, and the one least fitted to be exempt from the guidance of some wiser section of mankind." With such a discouraging description of the prospects, *The Spectator* went on to make a "suggestion." It was that the experiment be made, that the negro at some given centre be placed under the kindly government of men intent solely on raising him in the scale of humanity. It did not attempt to tabulate the excellent efforts that had already been made by many a Missionary Society, and the heroic sacrifices of a multitude of men and women who had laid down their lives in Africa. But it proceeded to say:—" That experiment has never been fairly tried yet, and we venture to suggest to the English Quakers that they should, as a body, take up the duty of trying it on a large scale, and in a continuous way." It went on to suggest that the Friends should purchase property and establish themselves on the island of Pemba, near Zanzibar, "where slavery, protected by our flag, assumes so frightful a form; and then set themselves deliberately to govern and educate, in the highest sense of the word education, the emancipated slaves. The result, if favourable, would so influence the opinion and the practice of the governing races which are now dividing Africa, that even a body like the Quakers might congratulate themselves on having accomplished an exceptionally noble work." *The Spectator* further suggested that negroes from the Southern States of America, selected by the Quakers of Pennsylvania, should go to Pemba and assist Friends in carrying out this work. It was a great responsibility to lay before a small community; but editors are often very liberal when they are dealing with other people's affairs.

The position of things in Pemba was undoubtedly serious. Mr. Donald Mackenzie, who had recently visited the island on behalf of the British and Foreign Anti-Slavery Society, and had brought home with him much valuable information, which has been widely circulated, estimated that there were at that time 80,000 slaves in Pemba. That estimate may have been too high, but the proportion of slaves to the whole population was undoubtedly very large. It was also calculated that 946 of the estates on the island were mortgaged by the Arabs to Hindu money-lenders. The issues involved were so vast, that a prudent community like the Society of Friends hesitated before they accepted such a suggestion. At that time there was a strong Christian Mission on the island of Zanzibar, but no Mission of any kind whatever on the dark island of Pemba.

John Morland, of Glastonbury, in *The Friend* of the 10th July, 1896, appealed for the establishment of an Industrial Mission on the island of Pemba. He said :—" The abolition of the legal status of slavery is not likely to alter materially the condition of the slaves, unless the knowledge of their new power is brought home to them by missionaries and traders, and unless proper courts are established in the island to which they may appeal, and officials to support them in their rights. To decree emancipation and then leave them alone on the island with their Arab masters would only be a mockery. Here there is a field for work open to us, and one in which there is a certainty of great usefulness." Following this proposal there appeared a letter from Francis W. Fox, quoting from Sir Lloyd Mathews, who expressed his opinion that the scheme for establishing a " Mission for the training of freed slaves in connection with agricultural employment "

BANANI.

H. Arnitage, Photo.

in either Zanzibar or Pemba was "very practical, and likely to be most useful."

On the 6th November a long discussion on the subject of the proposed Industrial Mission took place in the Representative Committee of the Society of Friends in London. Theodore Burtt, of Brandon Lodge, near Grantham, offered to go out to Pemba and assist in establishing the Mission. He said that it had risen clearly and definitely in his mind that he should offer to undertake the work. He had prayed earnestly over it, and day after day it became more clear that he was to give up his home interests and prospects and go to Pemba. He consulted his friends about it, but it all tended to deepen the call. Consequently, he laid the matter before the Committee. He felt that it would probably be right for him to take up a plantation in the island, and prove to the world that the freed men will work honestly and perseveringly for their living. Thus it would be an Industrial Mission with a distinctly religious aim. He believed that the way to bring the slaves to Christ would be through such a Mission, showing them in daily life what Christianity means of liberty and mutual service. He was a practical working farmer, and had had experience in handling carpenters', masons', and blacksmiths' tools. Thus, unknown to himself, he now recognised and believed that for many years the Lord had been training and preparing him for this very work. A minute from the Friends' Anti-Slavery Committee endorsed this offer. Caleb R. Kemp said he believed all who were present were pressed with a sense of the responsibility involved in listening to this proposal. Along with the responsibility was the privilege of sympathising with the one who made the offer. Our Lord does not withhold help and guidance when sought. While estimating the importance of our decision, we might rise to the privilege laid before us, simply seeking to do the Lord's will in it. Others spoke to like effect, and the following minute was made:—"This meeting has given its serious consideration to the proposal to take measures for the establishment of an Industrial Mission in Pemba. It has also heard with deep sympathy of Theodore Burtt's offer of service. Theodore Burtt has in person laid his concern before this meeting. The meeting has entered feelingly into the concern. It encourages the Anti-Slavery Committee to arrange for the proposed preliminary visit of Theodore Burtt to Pemba, and awaits the report of his journey before committing itself to further steps. The Committee is encouraged to seek for a companion for Theodore Burtt in his visit of investigation." Ultimately, the Committee encouraged the writer to accompany Theodore Burtt to Pemba, in the preliminary investigations, and both left England the last day of 1896, and reached Zanzibar on the 20th January, 1897.

Meanwhile a large and important deputation of Friends waited upon the Right Hon. G. N. Curzon, Under-Secretary for Foreign Affairs, at Downing Street, to urge upon the Government the importance of immediate emancipation, without any system of apprenticeship. Joseph Albert Pease, M.P., E. W. Brooks, and J. G. Alexander spoke at some length, and Mr. Curzon, in the course of his reply, intimated that the views expressed against apprenticeship should receive full consideration, and the arrangement afterwards recommended by Lord Salisbury was in this respect satisfactory.

General Mathews greatly assisted us in the initial steps on our arrival in Zanzibar. He sent the *Barawa* with us to Pemba, and provided introductions to Arab sheikhs. He also set apart for our use one of the best houses available in Chaki-Chaki, which he had furnished for our residence. Vice-Consul D. R. O'Sullivan gave us a cordial welcome and much helpful advice on our arrival at Pemba. Mr. Herbert Lister accompanied us in expeditions to various parts of the island, and by his knowledge of the people and of the Swahili language enabled us to gain the information required.

Another excellent offer of service was made to the Committee of the Society of Friends in April by Herbert Armitage and his sister, to go out to Pemba and assist Theodore Burtt. Both of them for some years had been working successfully among hundreds of boys at Leopold House, in the East End of London, in connection with Dr. Barnardo's Homes. Their offer was cordially and thankfully accepted by the Committee.

The Yearly Meeting of the Society of Friends gathered in usual course in London in May, and then the question of permanently undertaking the work in Pemba came before the whole body by report from its subordinate committees. The large house was thronged with Friends when the report was read in joint session of men and women. E. W. Brooks and the writer supported the tenor of the report. Mrs. Theodore Burtt and Miss Celia Armitage also addressed the meeting, expressing their belief that the Lord was guiding them to go forth when the right time might come. When the proposal was thus thrown before the assembly, the whole meeting appeared to be impressed with a sense of the importance of the juncture. Would the Society go forward, or would it withhold its hand? Not a voice was heard. In that solemn hush, many a prayer for direction rose to God.

After many members had spoken, Caleb R.

Kemp, the Clerk, read a minute expressing the deliberate judgment of the meeting. The minute stated:—" We have been forcibly reminded of the efforts put forth by Friends of past generations to rid England and the world of slavery, with all its attendant horrors and sin, and we recognise that we inherit responsibilities in this matter from those who have gone before us. We rejoice at the recent action of the British Government in abolishing the legal status of slavery in Zanzibar and Pemba, though we could desire that their action had been carried much further. This meeting has given much consideration to the subject, and after a full expression of approval, it empowers the Meeting for Sufferings to act upon the suggestions contained in the report, and establish an Industrial Mission on the island of Pemba, raising funds for the purpose. We trust that our friends who are practically interesting themselves in the subject may know the guiding hand of the Lord step by step, and that the Mission may promote the material, moral, and spiritual well-being of the inhabitants of the island."

The Yearly Meeting of Friends in London not only thus adopted the Mission as its own, but in the Epistle which it annually sends out to all its members and to its sister Churches in America and the Colonies it inserted the following sentences, calling the attention of Friends throughout the world to this anti-slavery effort:—" We rejoice in the steps recently taken towards the abolition of slavery in Zanzibar and Pemba. It is important that wise and Christian methods should be adopted in dealing with the freed men in those islands, and we are thankful that some of our members have felt it laid upon them as a religious duty to go to Pemba, in the hope of establishing an Industrial

Mission there. In this matter they have had the warm sympathy and support of the Meeting for Sufferings; and we have now authorised that body to undertake the responsibility of the Mission, and to raise a separate fund for its support."

Herbert Armitage went out to Pemba in May, 1897, to join Theodore Burtt. They proceeded to make inquiries respecting the purchase of a shamba on which to carry on the work, and ultimately purchased the estate of Banani, which appeared in many respects the most suitable for the purpose. It stands on a promontory, some four miles west of Chaki-Chaki. It is very fertile, and well planted with cloves and with cocoanut palms and mangoes. The shore provides excellent access for boats at all states of the tide. It is within sight of the Government estate of Tunduaua, where some of the English officials reside. There are plenty of excellent building sites on high ground in Banani, looking out to sea, thus catching the fresh breezes from the north-east or the south-west. There is a good supply of fresh water on the property. Theodore Burtt gives the following graphic account of the purchase of the estate:—

"On Monday evening, the 26th July, a note came from Dr. O'Sullivan, saying he thought we could buy Banani, and asking us to call and talk the matter over. So we went, and found he had seen the owner and offered to buy half; but Rashid, the owner, said he should lose credit if he divided a shamba, but he would sell all of Banani. At noon next day we went with Dr. O'Sullivan, the Wali Suliman-bin-Said, the Kathi, and Rashid-bin-Salim, the owner, to settle the boundaries of Banani. We were hindered first by the non-arrival of Rashid, and then by the Arab's prayer-time. On reaching Banani further hindrances occurred, and we found

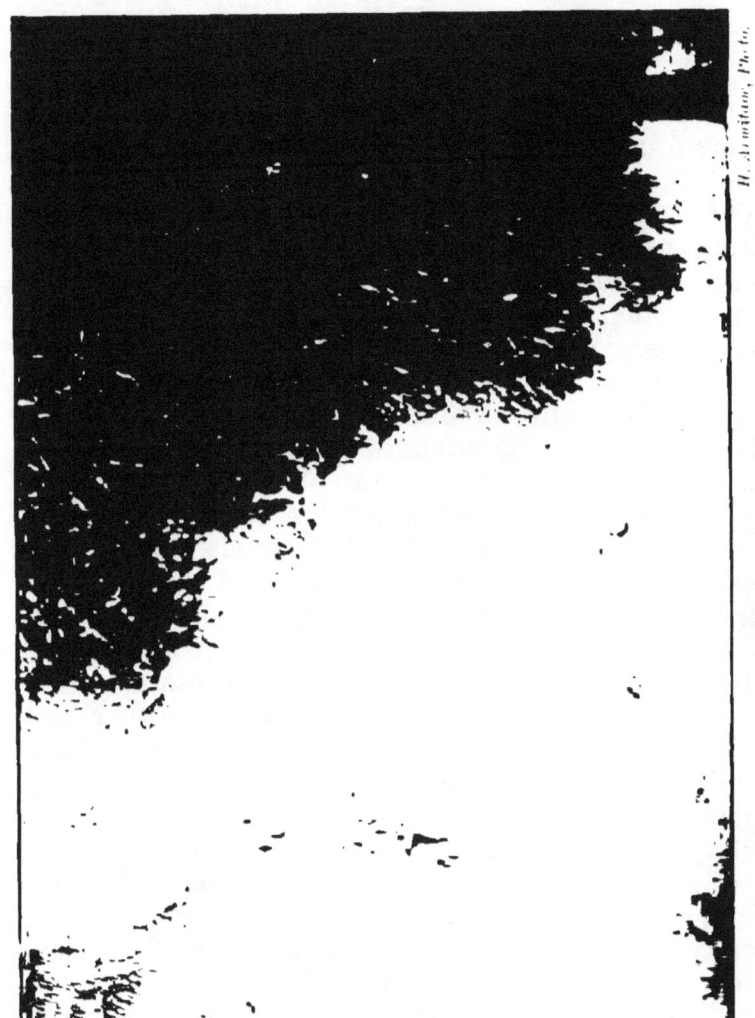

THE PATH UP FROM THE SHORE, BANANI.

that neither the owner nor anyone present knew where the boundary was. Eventually two slaves were found, one an old man who knew the boundary, and the other possessed an axe to mark the trees. Then all the neighbours were called in to state their opinion, and after much delay about thirty of us made a start along the boundary, which for a long way lay along a wet valley, nearly knee-deep in muddy water, and all covered with rank grass; or, where it was on drier ground, we had to force our way through grass 10ft. high, amid bushes and briars, among which probably no human being had passed for years. We were glad when our course lay along a footpath on the higher tableland. Many were the discussions entered into as to whom a tree belonged; some of the disputed trees were supposed to belong to a child, and so forth. We gave up all claim to most of the disputed trees. As the afternoon was wearing away we descended a steep hillside into another wet valley; but the Arab's prayer-time had again come, and a halt had to be made, of which we were really glad. Our followers at one time numbered nearly fifty, but now that the easy walking was over they dropped off, and when we crossed the valley and scrambled up a steep ascent, covered with tangled bush and briar, we were not more than half a dozen. Our work came to an end as we neared the shore on the other side, and we took the straight path through the clove plantation to the huts near the boat. Herbert Armitage and I took a quiet walk to see where a Mission House might be built; and when the Arabs had got through their devotions, and Dr. O'Sullivan had completed some business at Wesha, we got into the boat and made for home in the gathering darkness. At one o'clock next day we went to the Consulate to meet the vendor and the Arab officials. We rediscussed the question of price, the disposal of the present crop, the mud huts, &c. At last the price was decided, the vendor to be allowed thirty days to gather the cocoanuts now ripe, and four months to gather the clove crop. Then came the difficulty of translating the names of our six trustees into Arabic, which took a long time and much revision, and we dispersed while the short and simple deed was written out, to meet again at five o'clock. After further delays and corrections, the clerk rewrote the document in a most deliberate manner, squatting on the floor where the lamp and ink were placed. Then Rashid-bin-Salim-bin-Saif-Muscare signed the deed, which was witnessed by the Wali and the Kathi, and officially stamped by Dr. O'Sullivan as Vice-Consul. It was then handed over to the care of the Wali until we could get the cash (in silver) from Zanzibar, as a cheque is useless in this case. On Tuesday, August 10th, we sent word to Rashid-bin-Salim that the money was ready for him, but he replied that he was sick and would come next day, as he accordingly did, with a great number of other Arabs and their attendants. We met at the Custom House about two o'clock, a goodly number of people, and all who were specially interested in the business gathered together, and the money was carried in. The Wali produced the deed, which was carefully examined by Mr. Edib, who is a good Arab linguist, and it was pronounced correct and all in order. The arrangement about the cloves and cocoanuts and mud houses was again gone through, and the counting of the money began. It was in bags, all counted and sealed up at the bank. It was decided to count one bag, and if that was right the rest might be considered so. Accordingly, Rashid and four of his Arab friends and the manager of one of the largest Hindi merchant houses in Zanzibar and Pemba began to count the coin while we looked on, and all was found correct. But the Arab could not feel satisfied till all the bags had been emptied and the whole of the contents counted. We were glad to have it done in a way that gave entire satisfaction to all present. When the counting was complete, not a single coin was missing. The deed was then properly registered and stamped, and a copy taken to be kept at Zanzibar. It was a great relief to feel that at last the whole business was satisfactorily completed and everybody thoroughly satisfied. During the evening we saw a string of Rashid's men hurrying along, with the bags of silver, guarded both in front and behind by men on donkeys."

At the Representative Committee of the Society of Friends in London on the 3rd September, a further offer for missionary service in Pemba was received from Arnold Wigham, of Dublin. His brother had already served the missionary cause faithfully in China. This offer was endorsed by Friends in Dublin, and was cordially accepted, and arrangements were afterwards made for him to sail from Marseilles in January, 1898, with Mrs. Burtt and Miss Armitage.

In the autumn of 1897 Theodore Burtt and Herbert Armitage had the pleasure of welcoming to Pemba the Rev. J. K. Key, a missionary of considerable experience, who with his wife are now established in the north of the island at Weti, in connection with the Universities' Mission. They have secured an excellent site for their Mission House, and are organising schools and other work. Thus the cause of the negro gains ground, and one friend after another is being raised up for their help. A rescued slave boy on becoming a Christian said,

"THE FRIEND OF PEMBA" MISSION BOAT.

"Let us go to Pemba and ransom my mother, lest she die before she hears of the Cross," and in the same spirit of kinship with suffering humanity these missionaries go forth to rescue the slaves who have no one to tell them of a Saviour's love.

In looking forward, it is necessary to bear in mind that *every Mission must pass through its apprenticeship.* Errors in judgment may be made. Experience teaches how the work may be better done. Each year the comprehension of the condition of things widens, and early conceptions and hasty judgments become rectified. The oversanguine have to learn the truth of Mackay's statement, that "the heathen do not, by nature, wish the Gospel, although they sorely need it," and it is only by patient perseverance in well-doing that inertia can be overcome and satisfactory results attained in the formation of Christian character among the native races.

CHAPTER XIV.

THE WORKING OF THE DECREE.

"A thong gets cut through at the narrow place."—*Swahili Proverb.*

IN summing up the evidence that has been brought before us, we gladly recognise that the despatch of Lord Salisbury of the 10th February, 1897, bears evidence of a determination on his part to effectually abolish the legal status of slavery in Zanzibar and Pemba. His previous record in regard to anti-slavery inspires confidence in the integrity of his endeavour to fulfil the pledges that had been given to Parliament. The Sultan's decree of the 6th April also reflected the declared intent of the English Government. The proposal of anti-slavery advocates in England had not been to demand in Africa a proclamation of emancipation for the slaves on a given day, such as that of President Lincoln in America. On the contrary, the British and Foreign Anti-Slavery Society had pleaded for the abolition of the legal status of slavery, under which liberation would in the nature of things take effect gradually. It is, therefore, only fair to recognise that in this respect the Government conceded the main point desired. It was not demanded by the slaves themselves; they were too low down to clearly define their own position, and they did not evince that restless zeal for liberty that pertains to the free peoples of northern latitudes. The demand arose from enlightened philanthropists at home, and it was justly acknowledged by England, in assuming the government of East Africa, that emancipation must come. Lord Salisbury had gone a step further in the right direction, much to the satisfaction of the friends of the slave, in repudiating any suggestion for establishing a system of apprenticeship in lieu of slavery. For this he deserves our gratitude.

But, on the other hand, it appears to be a hopeless delusion to expect schemes of emancipation to be effectually carried out by Arab Walis who have themselves long been active slave-holders. Secondly, commercial prosperity will not return to the islands until free labour can be introduced without restraint, and so long as slavery is permitted to lurk in the islands free labour stands aloof. Thirdly, emancipation for the men which is not equally for women is contradictory and suicidal. Wherever slavery has been dominant, whether in Africa or in the ancient world, hardness of heart is a result. *The character of the slave-holder inevitably degenerates.* A slave is struck down at the caprice of his master. In Pemba an Arab bought a new sword in town, and wanting to prove it, on his return home struck a slave on the back of his neck with it. The man fell dead, and the master ordered the other slaves to "take him away." A little slave girl was tied by her hands to a tree stump, and the rope was so tight as to cause severe pain; the master, instead of untying the cord, cut off the child's right hand, maiming her for life. Usually in such cases no one dare give evidence, and the master sins with impunity as far as the law of the land is concerned. The Arab community to-day presents the sorrowful spectacle of a gifted and aspiring race sunk in the mire of self-indulgence. History proves, as Dr. Thomas Hodgkin stated in his lecture on "The Causes of the Fall of Empires," in

MOMBASA HARBOUR, FROM MISSION HOUSE, FRERETOWN, LOOKING TO SEA.

the University Hall, London, in November, 1897, that "The cancer of slavery is a fatal disease. One main cause of the fall of Rome was that the Empire was founded on slavery. So were all other States in that age, and all have fallen. The change in this respect is one reason why modern nations have shown much greater tenacity of life. Further, in all ages and in all places in the world *slave labour has driven out free labour.*" The fact that slaves do the labour prevents free men from working in such employments. In Rome the free man joined the army, or became a politician, and expected the Empire to support him. The slave class itself became disaffected, and was an element of great danger." As the axiom of Seneca ran, "So many slaves, so many enemies." Thus a free peasantry ceased to exist, and the slaves farmed Italy. Lieutenant C. E. Smith, late Vice-Consul at Zanzibar, affirms the same principle with regard to the African islands. He says :—"Slavery fails of its principal object. It does not insure a sufficiency of labour. Its effect is rather to hinder the supply, for its continued existence makes free men fear to come from the mainland to seek for work."*

But hardness of heart does not show itself only in slave labour. It is still more baneful in the family life. The harem shuns public gaze. Cruelty lurks in secret. As Dr. Hodgkin continued his indictment, "If we poison the sources of family life it inevitably leads to decay." The pure homes of England have made England strong. The vicious indulgence of the slavery of womanhood has blighted Mohammedanism. Our English Government must purge the Augean stable before society in East Africa can ever be reformed. It is perfectly right not to interfere with the domestic

* "History of Universities' Mission," pages 375-432.

life of the Arabs more than is absolutely necessary to protect the freedom of the individual. It is perfectly right to grant religious liberty, but it is utterly wrong under pretence of liberty to condone vice, and while pampering one race to leave another in bondage. Theodore Burtt writes, under date September 8th : "Many cases of cruelty against women cannot be described. The system of concubinage is used as a cloak to cover up slavery, kidnapping, outrage, and cruelty. A few days ago a young woman refused to allow her master to seduce her (probably as much out of fear of the jealousy of her mistress as anything else). He then said she should be his concubine, but again she refused and escaped, but when captured she was shut up. She is now lost sight of." Such cases show how unfit the Arabs are to have the option of concubinage when the women concerned have not the option of freedom.

The policy of a partial and half-hearted emancipation is one of the most suicidal that was ever conceived for a country that is absolutely dependent on manual labour for its prosperity. It shows how easy it is to mean well, and yet for good intentions to be frustrated. There are among the Arabs noble and straightforward men who desire to live righteously towards God, and to deal justly towards their fellow-men. But the whole tendency of Arab life in Africa for generations has been in favour of slavery. Can the Ethiopian change his skin, or the leopard his spots? Then may the Arab Wali be expected to administer justice between the slave-holder and the slave.

The way that the acting Walis at Weti, in the north of the island of Pemba, take charge of their prisoners is thus reported by a party of Englishmen who recently visited Weti :—" We found the tem-

porary prison. The old one was too bad for use, the new one was not yet built. We were admitted through a heavy door into a dark passage. We inquired, 'Where are the prisoners?' The gaoler pointed to a small door, saying they were in there. We again demanded admission, and after some delay the folding doors were unlocked and the gaoler stood aside. One door was thrust open (the other being chained). We inquired how many prisoners were in there? "Four," said the guardian of this place of darkness. Three Englishmen and a native squeezed through the doorway. So foul was the air, and perpetual the darkness, that neither the tiny lamp nor matches could produce light enough to reach from one side of the room to the other, though the place was only about 11ft. by 12ft. Just inside the door were the four negro prisoners. There was no window or other visible means of ventilation or light, the walls showing no signs of having ever been whitewashed. On the ground near the door was a mat, on which some of the prisoners slept; further on two men lay on the floor, making six instead of four. One was heavily chained, and complained of want of food, exhibiting his shrunken body in the dim flicker of the lamp. At the further end was a heap of decaying refuse. One man was suffering from fever. On returning to fresh air we inquired about food and water, and were informed that their masters or prosecutors sent them food every other day, and water was supplied when wanted. We were told that the chain-gang of fourteen persons also slept in the place at night, but this seems scarcely credible. We did not leave the town till we had reason to believe that the prison would be at once cleaned and ventilated."*
This was prison life in Weti in 1897. It shows how

* Visit of F. W. Fox and Theodore Burtt.

MISSION WORK, FRERETOWN.

Arab Walis manage things when left to themselves, and how much they need the oversight of Europeans. It is a consolation that the Government is now erecting a modern gaol.

Another illustration of the way in which the good purpose of England is being thwarted is given by Theodore Burtt in Chaki-Chaki, under date 4th September, 1897 :—" The sooner the British Government and the British public realise that the ordinary Arab official is incapable of administering justice, the better will it be both for the negro and the prosperity of the island. Last week I visited the prison here, and found three female slaves heavily ironed, who stated that their master had not given them proper food, and when they asked to be allowed to go into the town and find work, and earn money for their food and for him, he refused, and ordered them to go and work on his shamba. This they declined to do, and came and complained to the Wali, who forthwith committed them to prison for seven days, with shackles on their legs, for refusing to work for their master. On the Wali being questioned as to the cause of their imprisonment, he admitted it was for the offence stated above. When asked if this was not contrary to the law, he said he knew it was, and then remarked, 'But the women don't know that they can be free!' He promised, however, that they should be set at liberty at once; but when I next inquired they were still in prison!" These women were afterwards liberated from prison and sent to work for a Hindu in the town, the Hindus, as British subjects, being unable to own slaves. Theodore Burtt adds :—" This morning I heard that a woman had been sent by her master to work on another Arab's shamba. Having good reason to believe that she was being sold, she ran away and complained to the Wali. He called in both the Arabs, who protested that she was not being sold. The Wali accepted their statement, and sent the woman off with her new master. There is every reason to believe that this is a clear case of slave-dealing. But instead of the Arab official preventing it, he gave his countenance to the transaction." Emerson used to say, with much truth, "Light is the best policeman," and it is well that Englishmen are now on the spot to plead for justice.

A correspondent of the Universities' Mission in Zanzibar writes:—"I am glad to see some inquiries have been made in the House about the freedom of slaves. There is no visible difference here in the status of the slaves than there was before the proclamation was issued. Only this morning (August 5th) a slave was brought past this house in the charge of a soldier, to be restored to his master after running away. I understand that a slave who runs away from his master is quickly hunted down and put into prison for no other crime than a struggle for freedom."*

We trust that these repeated violations of the spirit of the decree abolishing the legal status will not be allowed to continue. The appointments already made of English gentlemen to supervise the decisions of the Arab Walis is a most important step in the right direction. One difficulty naïvely alleged by the Wali of Chaki-Chaki is that "the women do not know they are free." They do not know the provisions of the Sultan's decree, or how to avail themselves of it. It was not published in Swahili, the language of the people, but in Arabic, which few slaves can read. Several of our English "settlements" and missions have what is called "The Poor Man's Lawyer," that is, a man who

* *Central Africa*, November, 1897, page 189.

knows the law, and gratuitously administers advice and information. The poor slaves in Pemba seem to need a lawyer to disentangle them from the mesh which still holds them in bondage.

A necessary step on the part of our Zanzibar administration is that the prisons on the islands should all be placed under the direct supervision of English officials, and that it shall be no longer possible for local Arabs to thrust in gaol people who are not convicted of crime, and to load them with fetters at their own caprice. Such things are a disgrace to our Protectorate.

Africa is a continent of lapses from good resolves. Decrees are passed, expectation is raised, but the low moral tone sinks back into the mire. There is a back-water to every flowing tide. The Arabs enter into a covenant, but they afterwards turn, as in the days of Jeremiah (Jer. xxxiv. 10, 11), and bring their fellow-men again into subjection. There are many relapses, many an ebb and flow, yet the tide rises, and advance is made.

It is one thing to make use of every honest and competent Arab official wherever he can be found,—and there are among them many very competent men,—but it is quite another thing to hand over to them the local administration of a decree which is contrary to the whole tenor of their life. Lord Salisbury very justly said in his despatch: "It would seem desirable in any case to lend to the Zanzibar Government the temporary services of one or more British officials of special knowledge and experience, who should attend the courts and watch the conduct of cases." The officials who have been appointed require full power to act, and ought not to be hampered with restrictions. In nothing does the character of the English official stand higher among native races than in the administration of

MARKET, CHRISTIAN VILLAGE, FRERETOWN.

justice. Whether in India or in Africa, an English magistrate is justly regarded as the representative of impartiality.

The network of complications that a slave has to pass through in the effort to obtain liberation makes the recent edict in many cases inoperative. He has first to appear before the Arab Wali, who is, in the mind of the negro, asssociated with the prison and with shackles. The Wali in writing takes a full description of his person, his age, height, colour, length of arm, marks on the body, tribe, and when enslaved. If on Pemba, the slave must then be sent to Zanzibar, to be valued for compensation to his master, unless some official fortunately arrives on Pemba to give final judgment. After all these preliminaries and repeated appeals for freedom, a number of slaves have been returned to their masters, having failed to obtain manumission. How these complicated regulations originated does not appear. It was supposed in England that the appointment of Englishmen "to prevent injustice" would have obviated such maladministration. If emancipation is to be a reality, it must include the option of the negroes to return to the mainland. Where slaves have been well treated they are often content to remain with their masters. They wish to keep the same huts and the same m'hogo plots to which they have been accustomed. But they have the common proverb among themselves of the washerman's donkey that foolishly returned to the lion's den where he had been previously mauled, and the negro is not likely willingly to repeat the experiment if he has been ill treated, any more than the monkey who they say once rode out to sea on a shark's back, and, after due consideration, concluded henceforth to remain on dry land.

In view of the evidence now before the public as to the inadequacy of the Sultan's decree of April, 1897, which seems to have been received and ignored with much the same apathy as previous decrees of other Sultans, the time has fully come for a supplementary edict of full abolition of the legal status of slavery. Such a decree should embrace the ten-miles' strip on the mainland coast, as well as Zanzibar and Pemba. It should fix a definite limit of time beyond which no slaveholder can obtain compensation. The administration of justice on all questions between servants and their masters should be withdrawn from the Arab Walis and placed under the direct surveillance of English officials, who should have full power to free slaves. And, finally, freedom must be available for women equally with men.

The abolition of the legal status of slavery in the Niger Territories by Sir G. T. Goldie on the 19th June, 1897, in its simplicity offers an excellent example for the Sultan of Zanzibar.*

Whilst we thus urge the removal of complicated hindrances and nugatory clauses, we recognise that no despatch from London or edict from the Sultan can liberate the people from the customs of cen-

---

* The decree abolishing slavery in the Niger Territories was as follows:—

"Whereas a resolution of the Council of the Royal Niger Company, Chartered and Limited, dated the twenty-seventh day of October, one thousand eight hundred and ninety-six, authorises me to act in all respects on their behalf during my visit to the Niger Territories, and that all acts done by me in respect of the government of the Niger Territories and the affairs of the Company during that visit shall be taken to be done by the Council,—

"I hereby decree on behalf of the Council as follows:—

"1. On and after the nineteenth day of June, one thousand eight hundred and ninety-seven, the legal status of slavery shall stand abolished throughout the portion of the possession of Her Gracious Majesty the Queen of Great Britain and Ireland and Empress of India, which is known as the Niger Territories.

"2. The Supreme Court of the Niger Territories is charged with the interpretation of this decree by decisions given from time to time.

"GEORGE TAUBMAN GOLDIE, Governor.

"Asaba, Niger Territories, March 6th, 1897."

turies. That which changes the character and develops a new social order can alone effect full emancipation. The great emancipation which the African races need is deliverance from their own immoral and debasing tendencies. Lewdness appears as the original curse of Ham. It is sorrowful to think that the impact of the Arab masters has developed among the slaves the ancestral type. Nobleness of character and a steadfast faithfulness and loyalty to superiors crop out strikingly here and there. The children are often singularly winsome and precocious. But as they rise to the vigour of manhood and womanhood, the negro and Bantu races develop a sore lack of self-control. They are joyous and generous, they are patient under the yoke, but need a more robust manliness. When emancipation comes, they therefore urgently need the helpful presence of disciplined Europeans. A Government that ensures peace and justice is an inestimable boon. Self-denial for the welfare of others, such as that of African missionaries, lifts to a higher plane of thought the surrounding population. Even where the natives fail to assimilate the higher ideal, its presence commands respect and inspires confidence. Governments cannot afford to despise missionary effort, and it ill becomes missionaries to despise the valuable services rendered by Government. Christianity must be presented to the people of Africa as a life rather than a theory. A transfigured life is the scripture which the African can read. Unless our religion is effective to solve the problems of every-day life, it is not the religion of Christ. "I confess," said Bishop Steere, "I should like to see a brotherhood *cultivating the ground and singing psalms.*"* He did not mean that he wished mission-

---

* "Memoir of Bishop Steere," pages 333-336.

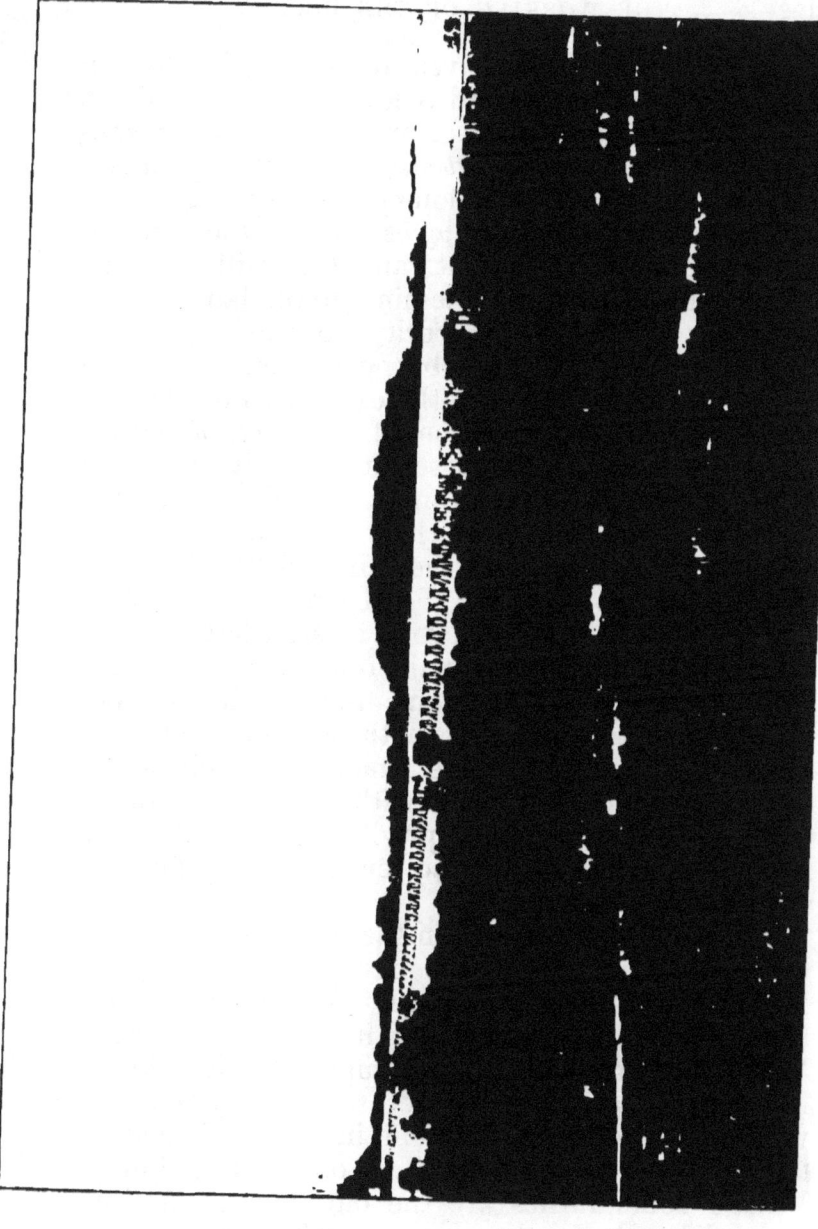

THE MOMBASA-UGANDA RAILWAY.
TEMPORARY TIMBER VIADUCT CONNECTING THE ISLAND OF MOMBASA WITH THE MAINLAND.

aries to devote themselves to digging under an equatorial sun, but he did recognise that "brethren are wanted who to a life of prayer and orderly self-denial *will add manual labour*," and provide general instruction as well as zealous preaching.

Happily, the price of cloves has for the moment risen about fifty per cent., and this will ease the severe strain that was coming upon landowners, but the return of prosperity to the islands is dependent on the Zanzibar Government acting vigorously with regard to the extinction of slavery.

Turning to the question of *remedial measures*, history reveals two courses as usually resultant from emancipation, the one an exodus from the land of bondage, the other the liberated race becoming possessed of the land which they had tilled. In Zanzibar and Pemba a third course is happily open—that where Arab masters have treated their slaves well, they will remain on the same plantations and in the same huts. The negroes form a strong attachment to those who treat them kindly. They also become attached to their accustomed surroundings, and, with the acquisition of freedom and the added privileges granted them, many will naturally elect to remain on the familiar shambas at a fair wage.

But we need to create in these islands a *peasant proprietorship*. With the exception of the Wa-Pemba and a few aborigines, the peasants have been crushed out under the iron heel of slavery. Valuable work has been attempted by the Church Missionary Society at Freretown, and by the Universities' Mission at Mbweni, in the settlement of freed men with their families on small holdings. Village communities are the old type of African social life. It is the type to which they must revert. Many waste lands await cultivation.

The Arab owners are heavily mortgaged, fruitful estates will from time to time come into the market, and opportunities will present for the purchase of fertile lands where cultivation has been neglected. If such properties were divided into a number of small freeholds or allotments on which freed men could settle, detailed cultivation would result in the increased revenue of the islands as well as in the consolidation of a higher social life. In the United States this problem came to the front in the South immediately after the Civil War. The slave-holders collapsed, and the slaves were free. From this dislocation of society we are happily delivered in the more peaceful surroundings of Zanzibar and Pemba. But the result is graphically portrayed in such works as Tourgee's "Bricks without Straw." The slave-holders said, "The negroes shall never own land." The friends of the freed-men said, "Yes, they shall." Yardley Warner went to Philadelphia, interested his friends in that city, and obtained money for purchasing a large estate in North Carolina. He cut up the estate into many small holdings, staking out streets and roads and space for public buildings. He let out the plots to freed-men only, and established a township. Out of honour to the founder, the citizens called the new town Warnersville. This experiment solved the question for the South. The men paid back the cost of the land by small instalments. Schools, a church, and a public hall were erected. The coloured people paid for the whole of their holdings; the town to-day is their own, under their own administration, and is an illustration of the excellence of peasant proprietorship. " There are now about eight and a-half million negroes in the United States; at the close of the war there were four millions. Their property holdings now

GROUP OF NATIVES, BANANI.
H. Armitage, Photo.

amount in value to $300,000,000. They have 25,000 schools and teachers. In their public schools in the Southern States alone 1,441,282 students are enrolled. They own $25,000,000 worth of Church property; they control many publishing houses and educational institutions. The total number of coloured physicians—all graduates—is 1,057. In the matter of occupations, 915,452 males and 318,331 females are engaged in agriculture, fishing, and mining; 1,640 are engaged in professional service; 524,594 in domestic and personal service; 63,367 in trade and transportation; and 72,048 in manufacturing and mechanical industries. The total number of negroes in all occupations is 1,895,432."*

Thus the coloured population of America has proved its capacity to enter upon the great inheritance bequeathed to it amid the horrors of civil war, and the native races of Africa on their own soil may yet prove their capacity, under the benign reign of peace and liberty, to play their part manfully in the destiny of nations. The cotton-spinners of Lancashire to-day little realise how much they owe to the negro cotton cultivators of the Southern States of America. Peasant proprietorship is a remedy to many of the ills that have afflicted Africa under slavery. The social security which English and German Protectorates are providing are the groundwork on which such a system can be opened out and resuscitated. The present Joseph Sturge wrote an article in the *Manchester Guardian* of 7th November, 1897, on the economic position of the West Indies, in which he drew attention to the advantages of peasant proprietorship in the island of Jamaica. The number of holdings under ten

* Statement by Booker T. Washington, Principal of Normal and Industrial Institute, Tuskegee, Alabama, U.S.A.

acres has increased from 43,707 in 1882 to 81,924 at the present time, and the report of the West India Royal Commission states that " the bulk of the peasantry are in a position which will compare not unfavourably with that of the peasantry of most countries in the world." The same happy results are seen as in the cotton crops which the Southern States of America yield since slave culture has been replaced by a system of small farms. The Royal Commission, therefore, places first on its list of special remedies " the settlement of the labouring population on small plots of land as peasant proprietors."

It is quite right for an Administration to check vagrancy, whether at home or abroad. But in checking vagrancy we must make provision for enabling free men to travel in search of work. Circulation is essential to health, and to bind men down as serfs to an estate is simply to perpetuate injustice. It would probable be premature to establish labour bureaus, but the outlines of some system, such as that existing in Germany for enabling men to find work, might be feasible. It is already a gain in Zanzibar and Pemba that under the enlightened policy of General Sir William Lloyd Mathews farms have been established at Dunga, Chwaka, and Tunduaua, where the growth of new products is attempted, and where the superior cultivation of existing products is encouraged. Free men out of employ have recently been drafted to these Government plantations until they can better themselves. Vagrancy, if unchecked, degenerates into idleness and crime, and centres such as these are therefore helpful to good government. The negroes need teaching the best methods of work. Slavery, with all its cruel limitations, has some recompenses to the slaves in this respect, that the men have been taught the rudiments of agriculture. But there can be no doubt that more complete provision for those who are out of work will be requisite as civilisation advances, and *the destitute aged and infirm* will require boarding out when incapacitated from earning their own living, and some provision must be made for them.

Subsequently to these preliminaries towards the new social order in East Africa may come the establishment of schools where the elements of technical education will be provided by the State, and a higher mental and moral standard evoked.

Tendencies are at work which absolutely prohibit the old order of things, and which must introduce the changes desired. The progress on the dark island of Pemba in 1897 is in itself an assurance of ultimate success. The appointment of Mr. John Prediger Farler as Commissioner is a great gain. Mr. Herbert Lister's previous arrival to take the oversight of the Public Works Department was also an advance. In conjunction with Vice-Consul Dr. O'Sullivan and his wife, and Mr. and Mrs. Edib, there is thus formed a group of intelligent Europeans who are intent on progress, and determined to withstand injustice and cruelty. The establishment of the Friends' Mission at Banani, where Mr. Theodore Burtt and Mr. Herbert Armitage are at work, and are to be joined by Mrs. Burtt, Miss Celia Armitage, and Mr. Arnold Wigham, is another hostage to the future; while our esteemed and experienced friends, Mr. and Mrs. Key, of the Universities' Mission, are happily established at Weti, in the north of the island. These arrivals are all tokens of promise to the people; and though it is too early to speak of results, we have no reason to despise the day of small things, but rather much cause for thankful-

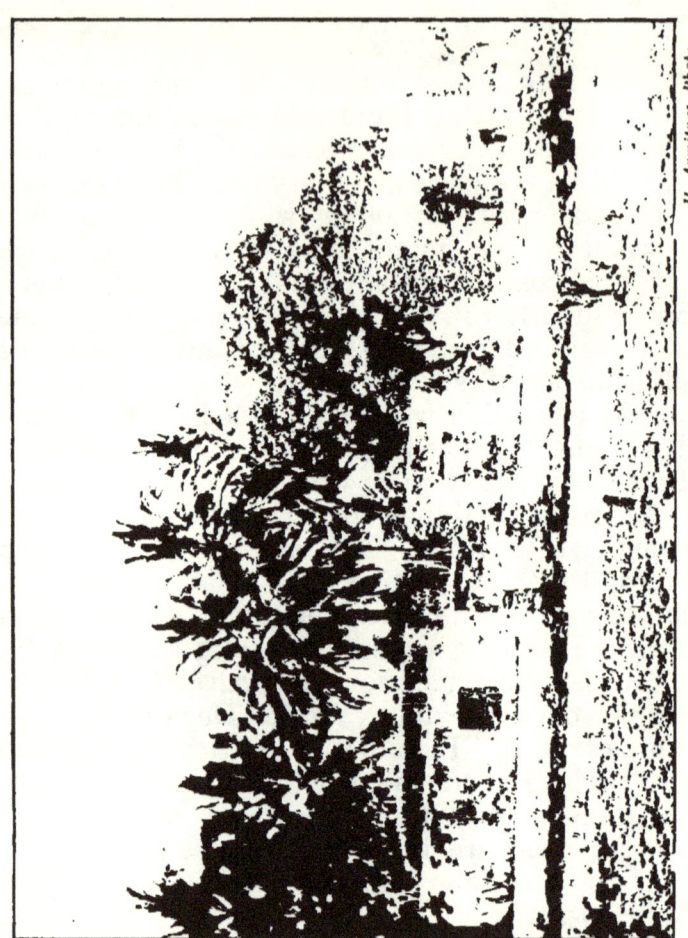
RUIN ON THE SHORE, BANANI.

H. Armitage, Photo.

ness and encouragement with regard to the island of Pemba.

Thus, while the arena of our discussion has been geographically limited, the issues involved have been far-reaching. Our attitude towards native races touches our relationships to Zulus, Kaffirs, Bechuanas, and Mashonas in South Africa, and throughout the vast continent. Why, it may be asked, has the zone of slavery been girt so long about the swarthy sons and daughters of Africa? Why were Northern latitudes the first to cast aside the heavy incubus of human bondage? It was that the free North might succour the children of the equator; that one freed race might with the light and energy given save another that had waited long for redemption.

William Lloyd Garrison's counsel to the people of England, after his victorious efforts for emancipation in America, are applicable to our position to-day:—" I have sought to liberate such as were held captive in the house of bondage. But all this I ought to have done. Henceforth, through all coming time, advocates of justice and friends of reform, be not discouraged, for you will and must succeed if you have a righteous cause. No matter at the outset how few may be disposed to rally round the standard you have raised, if you battle unflinchingly and without compromise, if yours is the faith that cannot be shaken, because it is linked to the Eternal Throne, it is only a question of time when victory shall come to reward your toils. So it has been, so it is, so it ever will be throughout the earth in any conflict for the right!"*

The Bishop of Ripon speaks of "the ministry of great races." There are strategic points in the world's conquest that call forth the heroic in national

* "An American Hero." (Swan, Sonnenschein & Co.)

200   THE WORKING OF THE DECREE.

life, and develop the knightly spirit that redresses wrong and succours the weak. The test comes to every nation in its appointed time. In the zenith of power nations are proven, not by selfish ends or aims, but by their action towards weaker races. The uplifting of humanity to its rightful inheritance on earth is thus gradually evolved through the united contributions to the common stock which Europe, Asia, Africa, and America each can render; that, with all their individuality of temperament, of character and service, all nations may be bound together in one great brotherhood, under the supremacy of the Universal King.

APPENDIX.

INSTRUCTIONS TO MR. HARDINGE RESPECTING THE ABOLITION OF THE LEGAL STATUS OF SLAVERY IN THE ISLANDS OF ZANZIBAR AND PEMBA.

No. 1.

The Marquess of Salisbury to Mr. A. Hardinge.

Foreign Office, February 10, 1897.

SIR,—The frequent communications that have passed between Her Majesty's Government and yourself during your recent visit to this country have enabled the Government to arrive at a decision as to the main steps to be taken by them in fulfilment of the pledges which they have given in Parliament for the abolition of the legal status of slavery in the islands of Zanzibar and Pemba.

Preliminary instructions have already been conveyed to you as to the general outlines of the plan to be carried into execution. But there remain, on the one hand, a number of important points of principle upon which you will expect to receive a more detailed expression of the views entertained by Her Majesty's Government; on the other, there are also a number of topics upon which, after consultation with the Sultan and his Ministers, you will be able to supply further information and advice. It seems desirable, therefore, that I should place on record a full statement both of the general grounds of action adopted by Her Majesty's Government, and also of their views upon the particular subjects referred to.

In deciding that the time has arrived when the Sultan shall be recommended to abolish the legal status of slavery in the islands of Zanzibar and Pemba, Her Majesty's Government have been influenced by the consideration that this is the logical sequel to the various steps which have been taken, under similar advice, by his predecessors during a period of more than twenty years.

In 1873 Sultan Barghash engaged by treaty to suppress the sea-borne traffic of slaves, and to close all public markets for imported slaves.

In 1876 he prohibited by proclamation the fitting out and despatch of slave caravans from the interior, and decreed that slaves so arriving at the coast should be confiscated, and that slaves should no longer be moved by land along the coast, any so found being confiscated and their owners punished.

In 1889 Sultan Khalifa concluded an agreement with the British Consul-General, to the effect that all slaves who should be brought into his dominions after the 1st November, 1889, and all children born in his dominions after the 1st January, 1890, should be free; and the former of these provisions was embodied in a proclamation.

In 1890 Sultan Ali prohibited by proclamation all exchange, sale, or purchase of slaves, and made provisions limiting the rights of inheritance and ownership.

These decrees indicate a progressive advance in the direction of emancipation, as carried out by successive Sultans, under the advice of the British Government. The present Ruler, who, on his elevation to the Throne, accepted the decrees of his predecessors, and bound himself specially to follow the advice of Her Majesty's Government in matters relating to slavery, will scarcely fail to recognise the expediency of signalising his reign by a continuance of the same humane and hitherto successful policy.

The best known case in which the abolition of the legal status of slavery has hitherto been enacted under the auspices of the British Government, and which has furnished an example for similar measures in other British Protectorates or Dominions, is the Indian Act of 1843. The first provision of that Act is inapplicable to the situation in Zanzibar. The second, third, and fourth clauses run as follows :—

"2. And it is hereby declared and enacted that no rights arising out of an alleged property in the person and service of another as a slave shall be enforced by any civil or criminal court or magistrate within the territories of the East India Company.

"3. And it is hereby declared and enacted that no person who may have acquired property by his own industry, or by the exercise of any art, calling, or profession, or by inheritance, assignment, gift, or bequest, shall be dispossessed of such property, or prevented from taking possession thereof on the ground that such person, or that the person from whom the property may have been derived, was a slave.

"4. And it is hereby enacted that any act, which would be a penal offence if done to a free man, shall be equally an offence if done to any person on the pretext of his being in a condition of slavery."

It may not be necessary that the exact text of these provisions should be verbally reproduced at Zanzibar, so long as the desired object is clearly provided for by the terms of the proposed decree, viz., that on and after the date at which it is to come into operation no court shall recognise any claim to the service of any person on the ground of the latter's alleged servile status. This must be the substance of the decree, the issue of which at the earliest possible date you will recommend to the Sultan.

Her Majesty's Government are fully prepared to recognise the fact that in tendering such advice to the Sultan they are bound, as the Protecting Power, to regard the legitimate interests of his subjects; and that, while resolutely pursuing the object which they have in view, they should take such steps as experience and foresight may suggest to secure the peaceful execution of the decree, the protection of lawful rights, and the avoidance of social or economic disturbance among the inhabitants of the islands. They have given very careful attention to the considerations that have been laid before them by yourself and other officers in the service, as well as by independent authorities, and by important associations who have greatly interested themselves in slavery problems, and the following are the conclusions to which they have been led by an examination of all the circumstances of the case.

The conditions of slavery in Zanzibar and Pemba differ materially from those which have prevailed in any other of the States or Protectorates in which the legal status has, either by the direct action or by the influence of the British Government, hitherto been terminated. The conclusions, therefore, which may be, and frequently have been, deduced from these cases, must not be too hurriedly accepted as furnishing us with guidance in the present instance, resting, as they do, for the most part, upon a supposed analogy which closer examination will show not to exist.

In the first place, the numbers affected in ratio to the whole population are, in the case of Zanzibar and Pemba, far greater than in any previous experiment, the total of slaves in the islands being estimated by the best-qualified judges as two-thirds of an entire population of 210,000. No proportion comparable to this was affected in British India in 1843, where it must be remembered that the Act did not apply to any one of the Protected States, but only to the territories under the direct government of the Company. On the Gold Coast also, and in the Malay States, which have frequently been cited as parallel instances, the total number of slaves affected was in each case only a few thousands, and those of an entirely different class; while in the case of Cyprus, which is also frequently quoted, the abolition was merely formal, and was intended to give legal validity to the termination of a system already dead, since it appeared that slavery neither existed, nor had existed, in the island within the memory of the oldest living inhabitant.

Secondly, there is an even wider difference in the nature and character of the system of slavery itself. Slavery in Zanzibar and Pemba is not, in the main, as it was in India and on the Gold Coast, domestic slavery, nor as it was in some parts of India and in the Malay States, bond or debt slavery. It is, on the contrary, for the most part prædial or agricultural slavery, the great majority of the slaves being engaged not merely in agriculture, but in a particular form of agriculture, viz., the cultivation of cloves.

Thirdly,—and this also is a condition not elsewhere existent,—upon this industry depend not merely the subsistence of the slaves and the livelihood of their employers, but the solvency of the State. It cannot be too carefully borne in mind that just as the clove crop in Zanzibar has hitherto depended upon slave labour, so also the revenues of Zanzibar depend in the main upon the clove crop, and that a blow struck at the one may react with disastrous consequences upon the other.

It may also be remarked as a fourth, and not less material point of difference, that whereas in previous cases of abolition this country has provided, or has had exclusive control of, the executive and judicial machinery required to insure, without possibility of interference, the execution of the change, we are dealing, in the case of Zanzibar, with a State in which the Mohammedan law is the municipal and secular as well as the religious law of the country, and in which the judiciary to whom the application of the decree will be confided is supplied not by the Protecting Power, but from the ranks of the native Administration.

For these reasons it appears to Her Majesty's Government that too much reliance should not be placed upon plausible but erroneous analogies, and that the case of Zanzibar and Pemba must be decided with reference to conditions peculiar to itself and upon its own merits.

Her Majesty's Government have been struck by the conflicting views which have been placed before them as to the probable or possible consequences of abolition. On the one hand, it has been strongly urged that, should abolition be decreed suddenly and without accompanying precautions, the majority of the slaves, naturally improvident and adverse to labour, would desert the plantations, and would either drift into the towns, there to pick up a precarious subsistence until they lapsed into beggary, or would migrate with their employers to Arabia or to parts of the African mainland where, under another flag, the servile relationship could be resumed; that, in consequence of this movement, there might even be a disturbance of public order and outbreaks of violence or excess; that the plantation owners, already heavily burdened by debts to Indian money-lenders, would be reduced to bankruptcy; that trade would be paralysed; and that industrial and economic ruin would threaten the State. It has also been pointed out that if the proposed abolition were to extend to the women of the harem and to the connubial system upon which the Arab family is founded, an opposition would be aroused that would enlist upon its side the stubbornest and most cherished convictions of the Arab nature.

Conversely, it is alleged that many, at any rate, of these dangers have been greatly exaggerated ; that when abolition has elsewhere been decreed (though under admittedly different conditions) no such results occurred, and that we must hope for the best.

Upon one point Her Majesty's Government entertain no doubt whatever, viz., as to the inexpediency and injustice of interfering with the family relations of the people.

So far from these being attended by any hardship, or being made the cause of complaint, it appears that they are very acceptable to every class of the population, the concubines who bear children enjoying a position scarcely inferior to that of a wife, and the children of such unions being regarded as legitimate.

You should therefore assure the Sultan, and invite him to repeat the assurance to his subjects, that no interference is contemplated with the family rights, to which so much value is attached by them.

Upon the other matters to which reference has been made Her Majesty's Government do not feel called upon to pronounce what could only be a speculative and conjectural judgment. They cannot fail, however, to be impressed by the fact that the less sanguine forecast is that which proceeds, with but few dissentient voices, from those authorities, whether officials, missionaries, or merchants, whose local experience entitles their opinion to the greatest weight, and that in the few cases where, either upon the islands or on the mainland, slaves have suddenly been emancipated in any numbers, or an attempt has been made to substitute free for slave labour, the results have not been altogether encouraging. When a large number of slaves were freed by the British East Africa Company at Magareni, they are reported to have looted the *shambas* and committed many excesses. It is as yet too early to pronounce definitely on the permanent success of the attempts to obtain free labour for work on the Uganda Railway, but it is known that when Sir Lloyd Mathews endeavoured both in Zanzibar and in Pemba to work plantations upon the free labour system, the bulk of the freed slaves to whom he offered a wage and land, after a short experience, deserted and declined to work. Moreover, in the last resort, Her Majesty's Government cannot divest themselves of the responsibility of the execution, free so far as possible from injustice or danger either to the individual or to the State, of a change which they recognise as being imposed upon the Zanzibar Government by the force of public opinion in this country, and by the direct counsels of the British Government.

These being the probabilities of the case, Her Majesty's Government have felt it their duty carefully to examine the various suggestions that have been placed before them for obviating the evils which it is thought in some quarters may arise. Undoubtedly the principal of these evils, and the fountain-head of any subsequent mischief, would be the disorganisation of the labour market in Zanzibar or Pemba, arising from any wide-spread abandonment of work upon the plantations by the freed slaves. Such a movement would not improbably be attended by consequences injurious to the public credit, as well as to the social welfare of the Sultan's dominions. It would seem, therefore, to be a principle of general acceptance that some machinery should be devised by which a too abrupt revolution should be avoided, and by which the continuance of an adequate supply of labour under the new conditions should as far as possible be guaranteed.

With this object in view, it has been suggested in some quarters that a system of State control over the labour of the freed slaves should be enacted, and that for a short term of years the latter should be compelled to work under contract and in receipt of wages, either for their former masters or for the State. Precedents for the successful application of this system have been pointed to in the case of foreign countries, as well as in

Zanzibar itself, where the slaves of British Indians were tentatively freed in 1860 by the British Consul, but were compelled to work under specified conditions for their former owners. Her Majesty's Government have closely scrutinised these proposals, and have arrived at the decision that they cannot in this case recommend them to the Sultan of Zanzibar. The experience of the so-called apprentice system in the West Indian Colonies of Great Britain between the years 1834 and 1838—though the two cases cannot be claimed as parallel either in principle or in application—was not such as to prepossess public opinion in this country in favour of any such intermediate stage between slavery and freedom, while the existence of a semi-servile class might be thought to impede the creation of that system of free labour which it is universally hoped may ultimately replace the prædial servitude at present prevailing upon the islands. A Government monopoly of the labour supply would appear also to be a condition not devoid of economic danger, while in the last resort there would be an element of contradiction inseparable from a situation in which the Zanzibar Government, while abolishing the legal status of slavery, should itself become, though for a limited time only and under materially different conditions, the official slave-owner of the islands. For these reasons it has been decided not to submit any such proposal to the Sultan.

There are, however, a number of precautionary measures, which, either in whole or in part, may, with probable advantage, be recommended to the Zanzibar Government, and upon the choice of which you should consult the Sultan and his experienced advisers. To check the sudden and uncontrolled desertion of large numbers of slaves from the plantations, and to anticipate any danger to public order, it may be thought advisable to increase the native police force at the disposal of the Government. To secure the continuance of labour upon the estates, and to prevent the ruin of the Arab owners, it may be found desirable to adopt measures by which runaways shall be prohibited from leaving the islands or from abandoning their families and occupations. A hut tax and the payment of a small rent for the plot of land occupied by the freed slave are suggestions that have also been authoritatively recommended. It may even be found that during the gathering of the clove crop special arrangements may have to be devised to prevent the disorganisation of that which is the main source of wealth and revenue to the islands. These are matters upon which Her Majesty's Government cannot claim to pronounce a definitive judgment, and which they would prefer to leave to the greatly superior knowledge of the Sultan's advisers upon the spot. Speaking generally, it is their opinion that it would be desirable, so far as possible, to refrain from experimental legislation, and to wait until the experience has been acquired, upon which such legislation, in order to be effective, should properly be based.

In one respect, however, immediate action should be taken. Whether free labour, in the place of slave labour, will, as is generally contended, be a plant of slow and reluctant growth, or whether, as it is to be hoped, it may at an early date take root in the islands, and be simultaneously assisted by a voluntary supply from the mainland, it would seem to be desirable to foster any agencies by which the risks of the intervening period may be anticipated or abridged. Hitherto the Indian Government have not been enabled, by the terms of the existing Emigration Acts, to sanction the recruitment of Indian coolie labour for the plantations of Zanzibar. You should at once resume your correspondence with them, and should inquire whether, upon the personal guarantee of Her Majesty's Representative at Zanzibar that the labourers shall receive fair treatment and wages, or upon conditions as to employment and supervision to be mutually agreed upon, it may be possible for them, as soon as the prevailing epidemic of plague in India has passed away, to sanction the emigration of coolies from Bombay to Zanzibar, where their presence may help to avert an economic crisis, and may successfully inaugurate the voluntary system.

It is the desire of Her Majesty's Government, in fulfilment of their Parliamentary pledges, that the decree which the Sultan is to be invited to issue should not be delayed, and the termination of the fast of Ramadan, when public business is recommenced, would appear to them to offer a suitable moment for its promulgation. As a short interval will probably be required for the effective initiation of the preliminary measures which have been sketched, the decree should only become operative after the lapse of a brief period from the date of its enactment. It is thought that for this purpose three months will be sufficient, and, accordingly, it is recommended that the decree should be put into final execution at the end of that time.

There remains a further question to which Her Majesty's Government have given anxious thought, and upon which they have not arrived at a conclusion without attaching due weight to the arguments that have been advanced on either side. In pursuance of a principle which I have already laid down, viz., that the lawful rights of the owners of slaves shall be protected if they suffer owing to the application to them of regulations imposed by the action of the British Government, and injuriously affecting their lawful property, Her Majesty's Government have decided, in concurrence with what is understood to be the strong opinion of the Zanzibar Government, that slave-owners who can prove to the satisfaction of the courts legal tenure of any slaves under the terms of Seyyid Ali's decree of August, 1890, and damage resulting from abolition, shall be entitled to receive compensation for such slaves. The terms of the second clause of that decree (by which all previous decrees against slavery and the slave trade were confirmed, and which went on to prohibit the sale or exchange of slaves and all inheritance of slaves except by the children of the deceased owner) were as follows:—

"We declare that, subject to the conditions stated below, all slaves lawfully possessed on this date by our subjects shall remain with their owners as at present. Their status shall be unchanged."

This decree was issued under the advice of Sir C. Euan-Smith, then Her Majesty's Representative at Zanzibar, on the 1st August, 1890, subsequent to the acquisition by Great Britain of the Protectorate of Zanzibar on the 14th June, but prior to the formal notification of the Protectorate on the 4th November of the same year.

It seems to Her Majesty's Government undeniable that under this clause a guarantee was given to the owners of certain slaves of the uninterrupted possession of their lawful property. It seems to them impossible to apply to the detriment or loss of the slave-owner, as has repeatedly been done, the remaining provisions of the decree, and yet to deny to him the protection of this clause, which was introduced in order to secure his voluntary acquiescence in the remainder. It seems to them impossible, with any show of reason, to argue that while the disabling clauses of the decree are to remain in perpetual operation, the enabling clause was only intended to remain effective until rescinded by a later decree. No later decree can cancel the rights which were publicly guaranteed by the Sovereign of the State, under the authority and sanction of the British Government, and no change or growth of public opinion in Great Britain can justify the repudiation of a pledge which was given with the knowledge and at the instance of the British Representative.

Such is the view of the case that commended itself to the late, as it also does to the present, Government. In a despatch addressed to you on the 5th May, 1894,* by the Earl of Kimberley, occurred the following words :—

"It will be your duty to recommend any further measures which may seem to you feasible for facilitating the total abolition of slavery without injustice to the Mohammedan owners."

In repeating to you this instruction, Her Majesty's Government signify their acceptance of it as a pledge of the attitude in abolishing the legal status of slavery, which the British Government have continuously been prepared to adopt.

It is not proposed that the rights created by the decree of 1890 should be extended to a single person by whom they cannot be proved to be legally enjoyed. For no slave illegally held with the knowledge of his owner should compensation be given. The application of the principle will require to be jealously watched and carefully guarded against abuse. No owner will have a good claim to compensation unless he can show before the tribunals, in the first place, that the loss of the slave and subsequent damage to himself are due to the abolition of the legal status; and, secondly, that the slave so claimed for was legally held at the date of such abolition under the various decrees and proclamations issued by successive Sultans. The principle of compensation is not directly affected by the controversy as to the number of slaves legally held, or the number of owners thereby affected. Computations as to the former vary between 7,000 and 70,000. Nor are there any data in existence upon which to arrive at a decision between the two extremes. There is no dispute, however, as to the fact that some thousands of slaves—although from the necessities of the case the number must be annually diminishing—are the lawful property of their owners, who, in holding them, have committed no offence against their laws or their religion, and whose claims it is impossible, with proper regard to justice, to ignore.

You should, therefore, advise the Sultan in issuing his decree to announce that he intends to adhere to the promise of his predecessors, and not to deprive any man of the slave to whom, under the decree of 1890, he has a legal right, without due compensation. It would probably be sufficient for the purposes of the decree if such a statement were couched in general terms. The amount given in compensation, which would probably vary in each case, and which should be determined by the extent of the damage inflicted upon the owner by the loss of his slave, is a matter upon which the local knowledge of the native tribunals will enable them, but upon which Her Majesty's Government cannot undertake, to pronounce. The system must be seen in operation before its efficacy or the reverse can be satisfactorily judged. It may be that the native courts will prove inadequate to the task devolved upon them, and that steps may require to be taken to supplement or to reinforce their action. It would seem desirable in any case to lend to the Zanzibar Government the temporary services of one or more British officials of special knowledge and experience, who should attend the courts and watch the conduct of cases; and you are authorised to make this offer to the Sultan, and to report to me your opinion as to the selection and employment of such persons.

For the reasons above-named, it is also impossible to predict the amount of money that may be required for compensation purposes, or the financial obligation that may in consequence be entailed upon the Zanzibar Government. Here, again, recourse must be had to experience for guidance. Her Majesty's Government are hopeful that the precautions which have been suggested may result in such a peaceful readjustment of the labour market, the emancipated slaves continuing in the majority of cases to work as free labourers, that recourse may not be at all widely

* "Africa No. 6 (1894)," No. 11.

had to the law courts, and that the claims for compensation may not be numerous, and may not amount to any considerable sum. Litigation should, as far as possible, be avoided, and means may be found in the majority of cases for a friendly composition. The courts will probably find in the dictates of common sense, with a due regard to the equities of each individual case, superior guidance to any that might be derived from principles of fixed or universal application. Upon all these points Her Majesty's Government are not justified, without further information, in expressing any confident opinion. But they recognise that, should the Zanzibar Government find its revenues seriously imperilled by the strain that is placed upon them in consequence of steps which have been taken in deference to the initiative of the Protecting Power, legitimate grounds may exist, as was stated by the Earl of Kimberley in his despatch of the 27th November, 1894,* for an appeal to Her Majesty's Government for financial aid. In such a case, however, Her Majesty's Government would require to be fully convinced that every possible means had been taken to verify the claims of those to whom compensation is awarded, and to obviate any possible collusion between owners and their slaves or the tribunal by which it is assessed, and to discourage a wholesale rush of slaves to escape from their present position in the mere expectation of living a life of idleness at the expense of the State.

In order to prevent the seizure of compensation money by the Indian money-lenders, to whom the estates of the slave-owners are in the majority of cases so deeply mortgaged, it would appear to be advisable to enact that any sums paid over in compensation for legally held slaves, shall be, like the person of the slave under the existing law, unseizable for past debt.

While adopting and recommending to the Sultan these conclusions as to compensation, Her Majesty's Government have not failed to examine the considerations that are commonly advanced upon the opposite side. The majority of these appear to them to rest upon a misconception identical with that which has already been exposed. It is, for instance, commonly alleged that the legal status of slavery was abolished without compensation in the cases before mentioned, viz., in British India, in the Malay States, on the Gold Coast, and in Cyprus, and it is argued that there can therefore be no necessity for the grant of compensation in the case of Zanzibar. This argument will not bear examination, for, on the one hand, it cannot be shown that in any of these cases had a formal pledge been given to the slave-owner with reference to legally held slaves by the Sovereign of his country, with the consent of the Protecting Power,—a circumstance which in itself differentiates the case of Zanzibar from all others, whether it be regarded in relation to other precedents or as a precedent in itself,— whilst, independently of that fact, it can easily be demonstrated that, on the very ground selected by those who employ this argument, the alleged analogy does not in reality exist. In no case does it appear that the status of slavery has been abolished in a Mohammedan State (where it is a part both of the civil and religious law) under a British Protectorate without compensation.

In India, as has already been pointed out, slavery in the Protected States never has been abolished. In Cyprus there were no slaves to be compensated for, because there were none to be freed. On the Gold Coast the form of slavery abolished was domestic servitude, as it had long prevailed, with no sanction but custom, among barbarous and heathen tribes, and as it continues to this day to exist over large parts of the African continent. In the Malay States, notably in Perak, where debt slavery was the prevalent form of servitude, compensation, instead of being refused, was offered to the slave-owner by the Government when the

* "Africa, No. 6 (1895)," No. 12.

legal status was abolished in 1884, and the freed slaves, under a system of apprentice labour, worked out a portion of this debt. So far, therefore, from any precedent against compensation being derivable from the cases here quoted, it would appear that the argument from analogy leads to entirely different conclusions, and that Her Majesty's Government, in deciding to authorise compensation in the case of Zanzibar, although that decision has been reached and is defended by them on independent grounds, have also been acting in accordance with the practice of their predecessors in bygone years.

These, then, are the points, briefly recapitulated, which should form the basis of the advice tendered by you to the Sultan.

1. A decree should be issued at once, abolishing the legal status of slavery in the islands of Zanzibar and Pemba.

2. An assurance should be given in this decree that no interference is contemplated with family life.

3. Her Majesty's Government do not recommend any form of apprentice labour.

4. Compensation should be awarded by the Zanzibar Government to such owners of slaves as can prove legal tenure of any of their slaves under clause 2 of the decree of 1890 and damage resulting from abolition.

5. Compensation money should not be seizable for past debt.

6. Her Majesty's Government will lend the services of British officers to watch the cases and to prevent injustice.

7. A renewed attempt will be made to procure coolie labour from India.

8. The Zanzibar Government should immediately adopt, in consultation with you, such measures of a police or precautionary character as may prevent social or financial disorder, and secure the successful operation of the decree.

9. Her Majesty's Government are hopeful that the change may be effected without risk and at no considerable cost. In the event, however, of a serious strain being placed upon the resources of the Zanzibar Government, they will be prepared to consider the question of financial aid.

It only remains for me to add that in indicating these measures for the consideration of the Sultan, of whose general assent you have already assured me, Her Majesty's Government have no wish to dictate the precise course which should be followed in each particular. Deference must of necessity be paid to the experience and opinions of His Highness and his advisers, whose great local knowledge will enable them to suggest methods of execution which it would be inopportune for Her Majesty's Government, who do not possess that advantage, to devise. That the legal status of slavery in the islands should cease henceforward to exist, and that the change should be effected without injustice to individuals, and at the same time without detriment to the public welfare, is the object which Her Majesty's Government have in view. They will await with interest your report of the steps which the Sultan and his Ministers may decide to take for carrying out these intentions.

I am, &c.,

(Signed) SALISBURY.

No. 2.

Mr. A. Hardinge to the Marquess of Salisbury.

Received March 29. (Telegraphic.)

Zanzibar, March 29, 1897.

SULTAN accepts the proposed decrees. They will be issued in about a week. His Highness' idea is to send for the leading Arabs from the interior of the island and from Pemba, who can all be here in five days' time, and to explain the measures to them himself. I am inclined to think, after discussing the question with the Sultan and Sir L. Mathews, that almost immediate operations would be preferable to even a two or three months' delay.

DECREE DATED 1ST OF ZILKADA, 1314 [ARABIC ELEVENTH-MONTH, OUR 6TH APRIL, 1897].

From Seyyid Hamoud Bin Mahomed Bin Said, to all his subjects.

WHEREAS by a treaty concluded in 1873 between Her Majesty the Queen of England and His Highness the late Seyyid Barghash, &c., the importation of slaves into the islands of Zanzibar and Pemba was forbidden and declared to be illegal ;

And whereas owing to the lapse of years and other causes, the number of slaves legally imported and held in these islands has greatly decreased, so that many estates have gone out of cultivation ;

And whereas the present system of slavery deters free labourers from coming to our islands to take the place of those who have from death and other causes disappeared, to the detriment of agriculture and of our subjects, who are thus driven to borrow money at high interest against the law of Islam and their own welfare, both of which are the objects of our deepest solicitude ;

And whereas the Apostle Mahomed (May God grant him blessings and peace !) has set before us as most praiseworthy the liberation of slaves, and we are ourselves desirous of following his precepts and of encouraging the introduction of free labour ;

And whereas our late predecessor, Seyyid Ali, in the decree in which he forbade for the future the sale of slaves or their transmission except by direct inheritance, declared that, subject to the conditions stated in that decree, all slaves lawfully possessed on that date by his subjects should remain with their owners, and that their status should be unchanged ; so that it would not be equitable to deprive them of any rights enjoyed under that decree without awarding compensation to their present possessors ;

We, therefore, having considered this question most carefully in all its aspects, and having in view the benefiting of all classes of our faithful subjects, have decided, with the advice of our First Minister, to promulgate, and we do hereby promulgate the following decree :—

Article I.—From and after this first day of *Zilkada*, all claims of whatever description made before any court or public authority in respect of the alleged relations of master and slave shall be referred to the District Court *(Mehkemet el Wilaya)* within whose jurisdiction they may arise, and shall be cognisable by that court alone.

Article II.—From and after this first day of *Zilkada* the District Court shall decline to enforce any alleged rights over the body service or property of any person on the ground that such person is a slave, but wherever any person shall claim that he was lawfully possessed of such rights, in accordance with the decrees of our predecessors, before the publication of the present decree, and has now by the application of the said decree been deprived of them, and has suffered loss by such deprivation, then the court, unless satisfied that the claim is unfounded, shall report to our First Minister that it deems the claimant entitled, in consideration of the loss of such rights and damage resulting therefrom, to such pecuniary compensation as may be a just and reasonable equivalent for their value, and our First Minister shall then award to him such sum.

Article III.—The compensation money thus awarded shall not be liable to be claimed in respect of any debt for which the person of the slave for whom it was granted could not previously by law be seized.

Article IV.—Any person whose right to freedom shall have been formally recognised under the preceding article shall be liable to any tax, abatement, *corvée*, or payment in lieu of *corvée*, which our Government may at any time hereafter see fit to impose on the general body of its subjects, and shall be bound, on pain of being declared a vagrant, to show that he possesses a regular domicile and means of subsistence, and where such domicile is situated on land owned by any other person, to pay to the owner of such land such rent (which may take the form of an equivalent in labour or produce) as may be agreed upon between them in the District Court.

Article V.—Concubines shall be regarded as inmates of the harem in the same sense as wives, and shall remain in their present relations unless they should demand their dissolution on the ground of cruelty, in which case the District Court shall grant it if the alleged cruelty has been proved to its satisfaction. A concubine not having borne children may be redeemed with the sanction of the court.

Article VI.—Any person making any claim under any of the provisions of this decree shall have the right to appeal from the decision of the District Court to ourselves or to such judge or other authority as we may from time to time see fit to delegate for the purpose.

Written by his order by his slave, Salim bin Mahomed.

(Signed) HAMOUD BIN MAHOMED BIN SAID.

DECREE, DATED 29TH OF SHAWAL, 1314 [APRIL, 1897].

From Seyyid Hamoud Bin Mahomed Bin Said, to all his subjects.

WHEREAS it is expedient to make further provision for the good government of our subjects in the interior of the islands of Zanzibar and Pemba, we hereby enact as follows :—

I. The island of Zanzibar is divided into three following districts (Wilayat), which shall supersede all previous existing administrative divisions :—

1. The District of Kokotoni, bounded on the north-west and east by the sea, and on the south by a straight line, which, starting from a point on the west coast half a mile to the south of Nnanjale, shall run to a point on the east coast one mile to the north of the village of Pongwi.

2. The District of Mwera, bounded to the north by the southern boundary of the District of Kokotoni, on the south and west by the sea, and on the east by a line which, starting in a northerly direction from Sungi Inlet, shall cross the high road from Zanzibar to Chwaka a quarter of a mile to the west of the village of Indijani, and shall run in a straight

line to the north till it meets the southern boundary of the District of Kokotoni.

3. The District of Chwaka, bounded on the north by the southern boundary of the District of Kokotoni, on the east, south, and south-west by the sea, and on the west by the eastern boundary of the District of Mwera.

Except where otherwise provided, all adjacent islands and inlets shall be held to belong to the District to whose coast they are in the closest proximity.

II. The city of Zanzibar, including Ngambo and the islands in Zanzibar harbour, is excluded from the jurisdiction of the Wali of Mwera, whose powers shall be exercised within it by our First Minister.

III. We hereby place over each of the Districts above-mentioned an Arab official who shall have the rank of Wali, and direct all Cadis, Akidas, Sheikhs, headmen, and other local authorities within the boundaries of the District assigned to him, to regard him as our representative and to exercise any powers now vested in them subject to his supervision and direction. All are to obey his orders.

IV. The Walis shall form and constitute in each of their Districts a District Court of summary jurisdiction, to be called the District Court, which shall henceforth be the chief court of the District, but from which an appeal shall always lie to ourselves or to such judge or public authority as we may from time to time see fit to delegate.

V. The powers of the present Walis in Chaki-Chaki and Weti, in our island of Pemba, shall be identical with those of the Walis hereby appointed over the island of Zanzibar.

VI. The following are appointed hereby Walis:—For the District of Kokotoni, to reside at Kokotoni, Suleiman bin Hamid. For the District of Mwera, to reside at Mwera Bridge, Serhan bin Nasr. For the District of Chwaka, to reside at Chwaka, Hilal bin Mahomed.

Written by his order by his slave Salim bin Mahomed.

(Signed) HAMOUD BIN MAHOMED BIN SAID.

INDEX.

A

Abdul Aziz-bin-Said, 55, 56.
Aberdare Mountains, 131.
Abolition in America, 7, 11, 194, 195.
Africa, partition of, 108.
Agnew, Captain, 154.
Albert Edward Lake, 103.
Albert Nyanza, 103.
Algeria, 104, 105.
Algiers, 104.
Anglo-German Agreement, 126.
Antigua, 8.
"Apprenticeship" labour, 114, 115, 167, 178.
Arab, the, as a social factor, 50.
Arab deputation, 33.
Arabs in East Africa, History of, 50.
Africa, as a market, 75; partition of, 104; future of, 105; British control in, 107; conflicts with aborigines, 107; compromises in, 108.
African, the, character of, 36, 38, 40; as a social factor, 40; education of, 147, 149.
Armitage, Celia, 168, 197.
Armitage, Herbert, 168, 170, 172, 197.

B

Balfour, Right Hon. A. J., 121, 136.
Banani, 159; purchase of, 110, 116, 170.
Bantus, 45, 49.
Banyans, 70.
Barakoa, 57, 58.
Barghash, Seyyid, 54, 95, 137.
Belgians, King of, 93.
Berkeley, Mr., 137.
Berlin, Act of 1885, 90, 91; Conference of 1885, 90.
Binns, Rev. H. K., 145, 146, 147.

Bismarck, Prince, 91.
Blantyre, 47, 158.
Boat, *Friend of Pemba*, 175.
Boats, native, 20.
Bomanji Manekjee, 68.
British and Foreign Anti-Slavery Society, 111, 177.
British control in Africa, 107.
British East Africa Company, 99, 125; liberates slaves, 131.
Brussels Act of 1890, 79, 93, 94, 99.
Brussels Conference, 93.
Burt, Rev. F., 10, 144.
Burtt, Mrs., 168.
Burtt, Theodore, 152, 166, 168, 170, 184.

C

Calabar, 108.
Canning, Lord, 54.
Cassava, 23.
Chad, Lake, 103.
"Chain-gangs," 61.
Chaki-Chaki, 106, 123; Castle, 64; Custom-house, 46; Market-place, 53.
Chamberlain, Right Hon. J., 76.
Chango, 22.
Church Missionary Society, 132, 140, 141, 142, 143, 144.
Chwaka, 14, 196.
Cloves, 24, 25, 100, 192.
Compensation to slave-holders, 97, 114, 117, 124, 132; opinion of Arabs, 33.
Concubines, 117, 180, 181.
Congo, 102.
Congo Free State, 49, 91, 94.
Copra, 26.
Corvo, Andrade, 52.
Courcel, Baron de, 91.
Court of Justice in Pemba, 82.
Curzon, Right Hon. G. N., 121, 134, 167.

D

Decree abolishing legal status of slavery, 114, 123, 201, 210; working of, 177.
Dundas, Captain, 133.
Dunga, 124, 196.

E

East Africa Protectorate, 125; efforts to suppress slavery, 95.
Edwards, Dr., 10, 144.
Egypt, English Control in, 105, 107.
Emancipation papers, 32, 131, 132.
English, the, as a social factor, 75.
English, the, in Africa, 87, 104.
Euan-Smith, Colonel C. S., 45, 95, 97, 118, 131, 136, 180.
Exports, 25, 77.

F

Farler, Mr. J. P., 14, 121.
Farms, Government, 14, 77, 196.
French in Africa, 104.
Frere, Sir Bartle, 55, 143, 144, 152, 156.
Freretown, 131, 142, 183, 186.
Friends' Industrial Mission, 159.
Fundu, 23.

G

Gallas, 129.
Garrison, William Lloyd, 199.
German Protectorate, 76.
Germans in Africa, 105.
Goldie, Sir G. T., 189.
Government by Protectorate, 87.
Gosha, 132, 133.

H

Hamoud-bin-Abdullah, 23.
Hammerton, Captain, 54.
Hardinge, Sir Arthur, 99, 114, 130.
Health, Safeguards to, 80.
Heanley, Dr., 29.
Hindu, the, as a social factor, 67.
Hodgkin, Dr. Thomas, 178, 180.

I

Imports, 26.
India, abolition of slavery in, 111.
Industrial Missions, 156 190.

J

Jairam Senji, 151.
Jones-Bateman, Archdeacon P. L., 152.
Juba River, 133.

K

Kedong River, 130.
Keltie, J. Scott, 45, 71, 109.
Kenia, Mount, 131.
Kennaway, Right Hon. Sir John, 134.
Kestell-Cornish, Mr. V. K., 57, 58, 71, 152.
Key, Rev. J. K., 174.
Khalid, Sultan, 56, 57.
Khojas, 71, 72.
Kidnapping of Slaves, 32.
Kirk, Sir John, 54, 55, 112, 115, 143, 153.
Kismayu, 137.
Kiungani, 149, 152.
Knapman, Mr. and Mrs., 154.
Krapf, John Ludwig, 143.

L

Labour, native, need of, 44, 63.
Last, Mr. J. T., 14, 121.
Leakey, Mr. R. H., 139.
Leopold II., King, 91, 94.
Lincoln, President, 177.
Lister, Mr. Herbert, 14, 33, 197.
Livingstone, Dr., 149.
Lovedale, 158.
Lugard, Major, 29, 31, 43, 44, 77, 79, 94, 157.
Lyne, Mr., 14.

M

Macdonald, Major, 140.
Mackay of Uganda, 71, 157.
Mackenzie, Mr. George S., 131, 132.

Mackinnon, Sir William, 131.
Matambwé, 65.
Mathews, General Sir L. W., 1, 9, 34, 62, 112, 121, 123, 132, 164, 167, 196.
Mbweni, 149, 152.
Mesale, 23.
Missions in East Africa, 143.
Mombasa, 10, 50, 121, 127, 143, 179.
Money-lenders, Hindu, 59, 70.
Mwanga, King, 138, 139.
Mzizima, Medical Mission at, 144.

N

Natural resources, 13.
Niger. 102, 108.
Nile, 102.
Nyasa, Lake, 103.
Nyondo, Isaac, 144.

O

Oil Rivers, 108.
O'Sullivan, Vice-Consul, 18, 33, 168, 170, 173.

P

Palgrave, Mr., 60.
Parsis, 68, 70.
Peasant Proprietorship, 192.
Pease, Joseph A., M.P., Introductory, 115, 121, 134.
Pemba, extent of island, 13; fertility, 13, 14, 17, 77; climate, 25; clove crop, 25; court of justice in, 82; slavery in, 29; abolition of slavery, 112, 177; Friends' Industrial Mission, 159.
Portal, Sir Gerald, 95, 98, 112, 139.
Porterage, 94.
Prison Island, 22.

R

Rabai, 131, 134, 143, 144; freeing of slaves at, 132.
Railways, 104, 135, 138, 191.
Ramadan, 21, 62.
Rashid-bin-Salim, 170, 173.

Rawson, Rear-Admiral, 57.
Rebmann, John, 143, 144.
Religion, Arabs and, 62; of natives, 40, 59.
Remedial measures, 192.
Ribe, 144.
Roberts, Mr. C. W., 151.
Rosebery, Lord, 86.
Rudolph, Lake, 103, 140.

S

Salisbury, Lord, 93, 97, 113, 115, 120, 121, 131, 167, 177, 178.
Seeley, Sir J. R., 87.
Seyyid, Ali, 55.
Seyyid, Said, 143.
Seyyidieh, District of, 137.
Sharpe, Mr., 158.
Slavery, transition from, 1; as it was, 29; England and, 29, 103; Mohammedanism and, 29; Arabs and, 33, 55, 81, 131; wastefulness of, 34; Zanzibar Government and, 37; and population, 40, 48; abolition of legal status of, 97, 111; effects of, 98, 117, 178; public opinion and, 111, 113; on mainland, 121, 133; and free labour, 136; Society of Friends and, 159; Rome and, 180.
Slaves released at Tunduana, 34; at Chaki-Chaki, 39.
Slaves, Runaway, 134, 146, 147; Children of, 98.
Spirits, importing of, 79, 94.
Spurrier, Dr. A. H., 14.
Stanley, Mr. H. M., 38, 47, 60, 70.
Steere, Bishop. 47, 112, 150, 151, 190.
Stewart, James, 48.
Strangers' Rest, Zanzibar, 154.
Strickland, Mr. C. W., 34.
Sturge, Joseph, 195.
Subject Races, Justice to, 86.
Swahilis, the, 43, 44, 51, 129.

T

Tanganyika, Lake, 103.
"Ten-miles Strip," 125, 126.
Thackeray, Miss C. D. M., 153.
Tozer, Bishop, 150, 152.

INDEX.

Tucker, Bishop, 112, 120, 140, 141, 133, 134.
Tunduaua, 5, 12, 14, 17, 33, 34, 124, 196.

U

Uganda, 130, 137; Protestant Chiefs and slavery, 140; Regents of, 139.
United Methodist Free Churches, 144.
Universities' Mission, 2, 149, 174.
Uvinje, 23.

V

Vagrancy, 196.
Vasco da Gama, 51.
Victoria Nyanza, 103, 138.
Vivian, Lord, 93.

W

Wa-Pemba, the, 74.
Warner, Yardley, 193.
Warnersville, 193.
West Indies, emancipation in, 8.
Weti, 20, 21, 65, 174, 181.
Wigham, Arnold, 174.
Witu, Sultanate of, 126.

Z

Zambesi, 102.
Zanzibar, city of, 1, 2, 78; bombardment of, 2, 57; Sultan's Palace, 3; climate of, 11, 25, 80; fertility of, 14, 16, 17; population, 40; conquest by Portuguese, 51, 52; Sultans of, 51; mission work in, 150.